Advance Praise for
My China in Tang Poetry

"Susan Wan Dolling has lived with Tang poetry for decades, and like the best teachers she knows how to make her familiarity ours. She tells the stories behind the poems, and her translations, clear and natural and fluid, have a sure sense of how emotions build and shine. Far more than an anthology, this series is a comprehensive tour of Tang poetry and culture with a genial, expert and witty guide."
 —James Richardson Poet, Professor of Creative Writing, Emeritus, Lewis Center for the Arts, Princeton University

"This book makes me want to drop everything and do nothing but learn about Chinese poetry! Dolling brings poets Li Bai and Du Fu vividly to life, both in her translations and in the stories she tells about 8th-century China, along with her own memories about growing up in Hong Kong. The notes to the poems cover poetics, wordplay, proverbs, history, geography, legends, folk songs, festivals, food, flowers, and more—everything you need to fall in love with these poems, these poets, and their world."
 —Laura Gibbs, author of *Aesop's Fables: A New Translation*, Penguin Classics

"Susan Wan Dolling's fresh translations of Tang poetry is a virtuoso performance...with vivid context and engaging personal anecdotes, Dolling's work interprets the Tang dynasty and its literary luminaries for a new generation of readers."
 — Kevin Peraino author of *A Force So Swift: Mao, Truman, and the Birth of Modern China, 1949*, Crown Publishing

"Susan Wan Dolling has given readers, from academics to lovers of poetry, a refreshing and innovative staging of Tang poetry. Informed personal readings accompanied by stories behind the poets and poems capture the enduring appeal of Tang poetry. In my many years of teaching Classical Chinese poetry, this series is a fresh take that is accessible to the general audience unfamiliar with Chinese as well as being delightful for the audience steeped in the tradition (and everyone in between)."
—Chiu-Mi Lai, Ph.D., Professor of Instruction, University of Texas at Austin

"Susan Wan Dolling's My China in Tang Poetry is surprisingly easy and entertaining reading. Susan's scholarship as well as vivid imagination shine through her storytelling and educated postulations, informative for both Tang poetry aficionados and neophytes. Her resplendent translations of the Chinese poetry are brilliant."
—Diana Lin, Hong Kong Journalist

"These volumes are a must for anyone who is interested in the Tang poetry which is the heart of the literature and culture of China."
—Margaret Sun, author of *Betwixt and Between*, Earnshaw Books

"Susan Wan Dolling is a scholar/poet who has breathed and danced these poems every day of her life. These beautiful translations are proof positive that translation is never a matter of just translating words. Thank you, Susan, for this gift of poetry."
—Nadia Benabid, translator of *Return to Painting* by Nobel Laureate Gao Xingjian

"In China, past and present, most kids grow up reciting Tang poems, and some even try their hand at writing these five or seven character lines when they feel inspired. Writing in the genre, usually poems of four or eight lines, might sound simple, but in fact it is not. As one grows older and read more and more of the annotated texts, one becomes more and more appreciative of the details of both the artistry and historical richness of these poems. As translator and annotator of these Tang poems, Susan Wan Dolling has done a fantastic job. The meticulousness of her annotations should be appreciated, and her renderings, accurate and smoothly readable (both script-wise and sound-wise) are definitely enjoyable."

—Diana Yue, Honorary Associate Professor, Hong Kong University, translator of *Flying Carpet: A Tale of Fertillia* by Hong Kong's own Xixi

"Best book ever!"

—Li Bai, poet and drunkard

唐詩

FLOATING ON CLOUDS

MY CHINA IN TANG POETRY
VOLUME II

温淑寧

Susan Wan Dolling

Floating on Clouds
My China in Tang Poetry Volume II

By Susan Wan Dolling

ISBN-13: 978-988-8843-90-9

© 2024 Susan Wan Dolling

Photographer: Clare Dyer

POETRY / TRANSLATION

EB220

All rights reserved. No part of this book may be reproduced in material form, by any means, whether graphic, electronic, mechanical or other, including photocopying or information storage, in whole or in part. May not be used to prepare other publications without written permission from the publisher except in the case of brief quotations embodied in critical articles or reviews. For information contact info@earnshawbooks.com

Published in Hong Kong by Earnshaw Books Ltd.

For my families in Hong Kong, China, England, Canada, and the U.S.A.

Contents

Basic Information   1
Preamble   2

Chapter One   Sleeping on Clouds (Meng Haoran 孟浩然)   11
Chapter Two   South Mountain Dreaming (Wang Wei 王维)   52
Chapter Three   This Music Knows No End (Li Ye 李冶)   89
Chapter Four   Waiting, Watching, Dreaming (Xue Tao 薛濤)   104
Chapter Five   Singer, Actor (Liu Caichun 劉採春)   128
Chapter Six   On Her Own (Yu Xuanji 魚玄機)   131

Endnote: Verse Forms   149
Poets and Dates   152
Acknowledgements   153
Epilogue   156

Basic Information

Some background information may be useful for those unfamiliar with the Chinese language in English. The dominant system for Romanizing Chinese used to be the Wade-Giles system. Wade and Giles were two 19th Century British sinologists. After the communist victory in 1949, a new system of Romanization of the spoken word was created, called *Pinyin*, which simply means "phonetics" in Chinese. The government of the People's Republic under Mao Zedong also created a Modified form of the written Chinese language, known as "Simplified Chinese", largely to make Chinese characters easier to learn and therefore promote universal education. In feudal society, the written language belonged only to the privileged. For the sake of simplicity, I mainly use Pinyin in these books. Exceptions are noted. For Chinese characters, I use the traditional or standard script (繁體/正體) because a systematized simplified script (簡體) simply did not exist in Tang China!

A quick word on names that come up so often in these stories. In feudal China, a person's birth name 名 *ming*, is used only by elders and the emperor. Friends and peers or someone in a younger generation call one by one's courtesy name 字 *zi*. Then there is the pen name 別號 *bie hao*, which can be used to refer to oneself or used by others among the literati. To simplify matters, I simply call them by the name (or names) by which we know them best in literature.

Preamble

My sister recently sent me ten poems that were gathered from a Hong Kong survey asking people for their favorite Tang poems. They made me think of our childhood and tugged at my roots. They are all familiar poems that most people growing up in Chinese environments know well. From children to hawkers and taxi-drivers to learned men and women, almost everyone can quote lines from one or more of them. My only regret vis-à-vis this list is that Du Fu is not included, maybe his poems are just too sad. Here are the poems, ranked in popularity from 10-1 with my English translations:

10 ON RETURNING TO MY HOMETOWN by He Zhizhang

> Left home a young boy, returning old,
> our dialect I kept but my hair's half gone.
> Village children seeing a stranger, come up
> running, laughing, asking "who are you?"

　　　　回鄉偶書　　賀知章

　　　　少小離家老大回,
　　　　鄉音無改鬢毛衰。
　　　　兒童相見不相識,
　　　　笑問客從何處來。

MY CHINA IN TANG POETRY

9 EARLY DEPARTURE FROM BAI DI CITY by Li Bai

We just waved goodbye to Bai Di's rainbow clouds at daybreak,
and here we are in Jiangling at day's end, miles and miles away.
Gibbon calls still ringing loud in my ears as I step off the skiff
that slid past ten thousand mountain ranges in the wink of an eye.

早發白帝城　　　李白

朝辭白帝彩雲間，
千里江陵一日還。
兩岸猿聲啼不住，
輕舟已過萬重山。

8 PITY THE POOR FARMERS by Li Shen

Under the hot noonday sun farmers labor,
drop by drop their sweat darkens the soil.
When you sit before your meal, remember
that each grain bears the mark of their toil.

憫農　　　李紳

鋤禾日當午，
汗滴禾下土。
誰知盤中餐，
粒粒皆辛苦。

FLOATING ON CLOUDS

7 GRASS by Bai Juyi

Green, green, the green grass grows,
a new year, a new crop comes and goes.
Wildfires may burn it, but it will not die.
Spring wind blows, and it comes alive.
Its fragrance breaches ancient roads.
Its liveliness splashes across old ruins.
Farewell, I say to you again, my friend,
as we gulp down the sorrows of parting.

草　[賦得古原草送別]　　白居易

離離原上草，
一歲一枯榮。
野火燒不盡，
春風吹又生。
遠芳侵古道，
晴翠接荒城。
又送王孫去，
萋萋滿別情。

MY CHINA IN TANG POETRY

6 SPRING DAWN by Meng Haoran

I had just dosed off and it's dawn
already — bird songs everywhere.
Last night, wind came with rain.
Any idea how many flowers fell?

春曉　　孟浩然

春眠不覺曉，
處處聞啼鳥。
夜來風雨聲，
花落知多少。

5 PLEASURE GARDEN ON THE ANCIENT PLAINS by Li Shangyin

Restless and in a mood, I went out riding
up to this garden with its celebrated view.
The sunset wraps me in a lavish embrace
only to say that night is fast approaching.

登樂遊原　　李商隱

向晚意不適，
驅車登古原。
夕陽無限好，
只是近黃昏。

FLOATING ON CLOUDS

4 ON FLYING CRANE TOWER by Wang Zhihuan

A bright sun sinks along the mountain slope.
The Yellow River flows endlessly to the sea.
If you want to take in the entire forever view,
do go ahead and climb up another story still.

登鸛雀樓　　王之渙

白日依山盡，
黃河入海流。
欲窮千里目，
更上一層樓。

3 QUIET NIGHT THOUGHTS by Li Bai

Before my bed, a patch of brilliant moon,
so bright, I take it for frost on the ground.
Looking up, I gaze at that brilliant moon.
Home fill my thoughts as I look down.

靜夜思　　李白

牀前明月光，
疑是地上霜。
舉頭望明月，
低頭思故鄉。

MY CHINA IN TANG POETRY

2 QING MING by Du Mu

Note: Qing Ming 清明 is a springtime festival when families gather to tidy up ancestral burial grounds and picnic.

Qing Ming is a drizzly time of year, on the road
people are falling over each other to find shelter.
"Where is the nearest drinking house?" I ask, and
the shepherd boy points to Almond Blossom Farm.

清明

清明時節雨紛紛，
路上行人欲斷魂。
借問酒家何處有？
牧童遙指杏花村。

1 THE WANDERER'S CHANT by Meng Jiao

Mother's loving hands have sewn
these clothes I wear far from home:
stitch into stitch on the eve of parting,
hope against hope I'll soon come home.
Tell me if an inch-tall grass can ever repay
the gift of sunshine in the months of spring?

遊子吟　　孟郊
慈母手中線，
遊子身上衣。
臨行密密縫，
意恐遲遲歸。
誰言寸草心，
報得三春暉。

FLOATING ON CLOUDS

Floating on Clouds begins with Li Bai to introduce Meng Haoran, and Wang Wei. They have all been called masters of detachment, Houdinis who can escape and disappear into the natural world, and thus may be sighted "floating on clouds". On the other hand, the expression can also be applied to those in love, romantically "floating on clouds". In the second half of this volume, we shall meet four "female talents", 女才子, as they were called, who engaged in this dangerous activity. A more solid relationship, friendship, being a main theme in Chinese poetry, is also found throughout this volume.

Before we meet these Tang poets, however, let me introduce you to a poet-recluse and the original master of detachment, admired by all. He is Tao Yuanming 陶淵明 (365-427) who gave himself the courtesy name of Tao Qian 陶潛 when he went into hiding or reclusion during the fall of the Jin dynasty which ended in 420. Growing up, we referred to him by both names without giving them much thought. Now, I am fascinated. Let me take you on a quick detour into the meaning of the very interesting name his father gave him at birth and how it foreshadowed the courtesy name he made up for himself. The first character in his given name, Yuan 淵, is a pictograph, one of six types of Chinese characters and the oldest way of forming them.

[A word of caution: the following is NOT an argument for ideographic reading of the Chinese character. The use of pictographs is only one of six ways to form a Chinese character, the most primitive way. Pictographic characters are found on oracle bones as early as the 14th – 11th Centuries BCE.] The word *yuan* 淵, is made up of a water radical and a drawing that look like the shores (the two long strokes on the sides) with what looks like a maze in the middle. Thus, it means something hard to fathom. The second character in his birth name is ming 明. It is

MY CHINA IN TANG POETRY

made up of a sun and a moon, meaning "bright", and eventually evolving to mean "to understand", very much like the lightbulb idea in our cartoons. In other words, this boy is supposed to be able to understand and therefore illuminate deep thoughts. The boy's father had some foresight. Then, when it came time for Yuanming to give himself a courtesy name, he chose the word qian 潛, which means to submerge, or hide, which was what he was doing, hiding from the authorities, and it also echoes his birth name: to deep dive for the truth. In fact, one's courtesy name is conventionally an echo of the birth name, but in this case, the practice is made doubly meaningful in that Tao Qian became a recluse. To keep things simple, we shall refer to him by his chosen name of Tao Qian in this volume.

In Chinese literature, he is called the father of "Fields and Gardens Poetry", *tian yuan shi*, 田園詩. We might call "Fields and Gardens" the domestic side of "Mountains and Streams Poetry", *shan shui shi*, 山水詩, and the father of this latter genre is Xie Lingyun 謝靈運 (385-433) also of the Six Dynasties Era. Those were dangerous times, even more dangerous than the Tang dynasty, and Xie's fate was somewhat different from Tao's. Whereas Tao had the wisdom to withdraw from politics, Xie stayed on, and was exiled many times and, in the end, executed. He had many posthumous admirers too, but the wise Tao Qian had even more. Tao famously proclaimed that he was "not going to bend his waist [bow his head] for five bushels of rice [a government salary]", when he went into hiding. The following is his most famous poem, so much so that after it became known among poets, the very mention of thatch hut, chrysanthemums, South Mountain, eastern hedge, and forgetting words, or even drinking wine, cannot be mentioned without calling up his ghost.

FLOATING ON CLOUDS

DRINKING SONG #5

I built a thatch hut in the hubbub of men,
but the noise of their traffic I do not hear.
You ask how that can be?
Nature favors the mind detached.
Picking chrysanthemums at the eastern hedge,
greeting South Mountain standing before me,
day and night, mountain air clears the mind,
as birds fly past, coming and going naturally.
Truth is right here for the asking,
only words escape, debate amiss.

飲酒・其五

結廬在人境，
而無車馬喧。
問君何能爾？
心遠地自偏。
采菊東籬下，
悠然見南山。
山氣日夕佳，
飛鳥相與還。
此中有真意，
欲辨已忘言。

1

Meng Haoran 孟浩然 (689/91 – 740)
Sleeping On Clouds

SPRING DAWN

I had just dosed off and it's dawn
already — bird songs everywhere.
Last night, wind came with rain.
Any idea how many flowers fell?

春曉

春眠不覺曉，
處處聞啼鳥。
夜來風雨聲，
花落知多少。

I paid little attention to Meng Haoran when I reclaimed Chinese poetry as an adult, just as I was not much aware of him when I was first introduced to the Tang poets at school. Sure, I knew he was a famous Tang poet who wrote a much loved four-line poem about taking a nap on a spring evening and waking up at dawn, but my memory of him was as short and mysterious as the above *jueju* 絕句. (See Endnote for definition of all verse forms.) I did not understand his fame or his charm. Lately, I have come to appreciate him more and more, and if I were to put together a volume of his poetry, I would call it 'The Recluse with a Thousand Friends'. His reputation may be that of a recluse, but the personality that comes through his poetry is that of an easygoing, warm, and generous friend. Li Bai, one of the superstars in Volume I, was twelve years his junior, and knew Meng by reputation, admired his poetry, and was sympathetic to his difficulties in finding a position at court. Meng's farm was not far from Anlu where Li Bai settled down on and off for about ten years. Li Bai had visited Meng once before he got married, when he heard that Meng had given up the elusive pursuit of officialdom and went home to his "garden and field", which happened to have been within sight of South Mountain. In Li Bai's romantic imagination, this return home must have been equivalent to Tao Qian's "hiding". In reality, Meng's family owned a small farm, and since his parents were old and he was getting nowhere in his political pursuit, Meng decided to go home and look after them, at least for a while. The two poets met for the first time in 727 or 728. Li Bai was twenty-six and Meng forty, and just like Li Bai and Du Fu seventeen years later, they were "old friends on first meeting" 一見如故. Later, in 734 or 735, when he heard Meng was getting ready to leave for Yangzhou, Li Bai quickly sent him a message for them to meet at Gold Crane Tower, where they could spend some time together at that scenic spot and say goodbye.

When he had passed by Gold Crane Tower the first time on his way to the coast, Li Bai had seen and envied Cui Hao's famous poem by that name and had ever since tried to surpass it. (Cui Hao was Li Bai's contemporary; his dates are c.704-754. He was just a couple of years younger than Li Bai, but the two never met). After that initial visit, Gold Crane Tower found its way into almost fifty of Li's poems that we know of. He was somewhat preoccupied with the place, the story, and Cui Hao's poem.

The Story of Gold Crane Tower 黃鶴樓

黃鶴樓 *huang he lou*, is often translated as Yellow Crane Tower. The word for yellow 黃 in Chinese, however, can mean gold, as in yellow metal 黃金, or earth, as in yellow earth 黃土, and thus, as a color it covers a wide range of possibilities, from yellow to gold to brown. I am choosing gold here both for its sound and for this story's mythological context. Gold Crane Tower has been in existence as far back as we can trace to 223 CE. The original tower is said to have been built as a watch tower by Sun Quan, one of the three kings of the Three Kingdoms (222-280). Since then, it has been destroyed and built many times over. In 1884, it was burned down completely and was not rebuilt until the 1980's. It has been a tourist attraction for a long time.

When Li Bai arrived on the scene in the 700's, a custom had grown up around it for tourists who had the talent, or thought they did, to leave poems about the tower on the walls. As the story goes, our young poet had climbed up to the top, ready to perform, when he saw Cui Hao's poem and decided another was unnecessary.

The best known among the various legends that tell the story of the origin of Gold Crane Tower is that of a wine merchant. The man's name was Xin. One day, an old pauper wandered into his wine shop, and without hesitation, he offered the poor man respite, food, and wine. The pauper came back day after day for several years, and Xin treated him in the same way every time, with hospitality and respect. Some time later, on his way out, the old man picked up some orange peel and drew a picture of a crane on the wall.

He told Xin that he only had to clap his hands and the crane would leap off the wall and do a dance for him. Then the old man went away. Eventually, the dancing crane brought so much business to the wine shop that Xin became a wealthy man. Another ten years went by and one day the old man reappeared. He started playing on a flute and the crane came off the wall, whereupon the old man rode off on its back into the clouds. They never returned. Xin then built the Gold Crane Tower to commemorate the immortal whose name was Zi'an, or so they say.

As with any other tourist, this was the story Li Bai knew. When he climbed to the top of the tower, he must have read a few of the inferior poems other tourists left on the wall, and was ready to outshine them, when he came upon Cui Hao's poem. After reading it, he apparently said, "There is no reason for writing another poem unless it is better than Cui Hao's." Thus, he never did write another poem called "Gold Crane Tower", even though he mentioned and alluded to it numerous times in his poetry.

GOLD CRANE TOWER by Cui Hao 崔浩

> He came long ago and left on his golden crane,
> all that remains is this empty Gold Crane Tower.
> The gold crane has gone away, never to return:
> a thousand years, white clouds in an empty sky.
> Too green the green trees of old Hanyang,
> Too sweet the sweet grass of Parrot Island.
> Daylight recedes with hope for home. Mist
> heavy on the water. Sadness fills my heart.

MY CHINA IN TANG POETRY

黃鶴樓

昔人已乘黃鶴去，
此地空餘黃鶴樓。
黃鶴一去不復返，
白雲千載空悠悠。
晴川歷歷漢陽樹，
芳草萋萋鸚鵡洲。
日暮鄉關何處是？
煙波江上使人愁。

Now for the Li Bai poem. Many readers interpret the next poem as a happy farewell in a flourishing time of year, during a prosperous era in history, coming from a yet-to-be disillusioned young poet. I found it a bit sad. As Du Fu would say of Li Bai in "At Sky's End: Li Bai on my Mind", "Goodbyes have always been hard for [him]." Also, I am, perhaps reading it retrospectively. A few years later, in 739, on his way back from the east, Li Bai thought he would visit Meng again when he passed through Xiangyang, but Meng was not home. A year later, Meng was to die after a party with another friend. As the story goes, Wang Changling was visiting from out of town. They had not seen each other for a while, and in his excitement to entertain his friend, Meng forgot that his healer told him to avoid seafood until the chronic sore on his back was cured. He prepared a feast, which included the famous Xiangyang bream for his friend and could not refrain from taking a few bites himself, which, unfortunately, did him in. He was only fifty-one, but in Tang China, he would have been considered an old man. This good-bye meeting on Snake Hill at Gold Crane Tower, one of the four great towers of China, turned out to be the last of their good times together. Some say he has finally bested Cui Hao's poem with this one.

What do you think? For myself, I find this a very different poem from Cui Hao's "Gold Crane Tower" in theme, in style, and in form. I don't see how one can be "better" than the other.

SEEING OFF MENG HAORAN ON HIS WAY TO YANGZHOU

We said goodbye, my old friend and I, at Gold Crane Tower.
Mid-spring flowers will escort him all the way to Yangzhou,
I followed the distant reflection of his lone sail to sky's end,
and watched it drop off the Great River's smoky blue horizon.

黃鶴樓送孟浩然之廣陵

故人西辭黃鶴樓，
煙花三月下揚州。
孤帆遠影碧空盡，
唯見長江天際流。

"Mid-spring" is my substitute for "the third lunar month" in the Chinese, when flowers are newly bloomed, almost full but not so full that they have begun to fall. Also, Yangzhou 揚州 was where Meng was heading. The Great River is Changjiang 長江 or the Yangtze. Guangling 廣陵, mentioned in the Chinese title, is another name for Yangzhou.

———∽∽∽———

Li Bai's endearing poem, "For Meng Haoran," was not written after Meng's death, but rather soon after they met for the first time, although it sounds much like a eulogy.

MY CHINA IN TANG POETRY

FOR MENG HAORAN

I love old Master Meng with all my heart.
Unbound by conventions, he has no equal.
In youth, he forsook cap and carriage, now
he rests his white head on floating clouds.
Elegant like his friend, the drunken moon,
he chooses to cultivate flowers over kings.
Highest peaks bow to him to show respect:
I press my palms together and follow suit.

贈孟浩然

吾愛孟夫子，
風流天下聞。
紅顏棄軒冕，
白首臥松雲。
醉月頻中聖，
迷花不事君。
高山安可仰，
徒此揖清芬。

If you think this portrait of Meng sounds suspiciously like one Li Bai might have wished a younger poet to write about him, you would probably be right, though Li Bai was not yet ready to "[forsake] cap and carriage" at the time. As with so many Chinese poet-scholars of their era, Li Bai may have admired the lofty goals of reclusion, but the pull towards worldly recognition and service to country was strong enough to keep him from giving it up altogether, and as we have seen in *Superstars*, Li Bai struggled with this contradiction to the very end of his life.

FLOATING ON CLOUDS

Seven Sages of the Bamboo Grove 竹林七賢

These seven third century eccentric intellectuals have been compared to 1960s Hippies in America by the authors of *Flashback History* (Stewart Lee Beck and Katie Lu, China Simplified Inc., 2017). The comparison makes sense, as these bamboo grove gatherers are as counterculture as they come. In their case, the culture they were countering was the conspiracy-prone, corrupt, and confining extreme-Confucianism in the post-Han dynasty chaos, that is, the turbulent years of the early Western Jin dynasty (265–317). Rather than submitting to or fighting those in power, these men chose to gather at a bamboo grove on their leader's property to drink, make poetry, philosophize and sing the praises of the simple, rustic life. They were also a group that formed what is called "forgotten years friendships", a multigenerational community made up of teenagers to older adults. The group have become a legendary ideal, and some have questioned whether the individual members actually all lived during the same years. In any case, they were supposed to have subscribed to the Daoist belief in spontaneity and the celebration of nature. Their musical instrument of choice was the *guqin*, or simply, the *qin*, a zither-like instrument often mentioned in the poetry in this volume. Unsurprisingly, Meng Haoran and Li Bai were both admirers of these sages. Indeed, these Seven Sages of the Bamboo Grove have been quoted and alluded to by poets ever since their existence and were much admired by many Tang dynasty poets. As the following poem attests, Meng Haoran had his own bamboo grove gatherings in his brother Xiran's back yard.

MY CHINA IN TANG POETRY

AT MY BROTHER XIRAN'S BAMBOO KIOSK

You and I and these two, three brothers here
have known each other as only best friends can,
with hope in our hearts like wild geese soaring in the sky,
and love for each other like attentive wagtails in the sand.
Talking poetry and sharing ideas like the Seven Sages
used to do, in the serenity of our own bamboo grove.
And how we enjoy the wine and spontaneous music,
when we feel moved to play a few tunes on the qin.

洗然弟竹亭

吾與二三子，
平生结交深。
俱懷鴻鵠志，
昔有鶺鴒心。
逸氣假毫翰，
清風在竹林。
達是酒中趣，
琴上偶然音。

Friendship, ambition (wild geese here), brotherly love (wagtails), poetic community, escape from hypocrisy and intrigue (Seven Sages), drinking, and spontaneity, are recurring themes all through Meng's life. The most pronounced difference between the early and late poems is his letting go of the soaring geese and easing into the Tao Qian state of mind.

Poets of his own generation and those who came after him admire Meng Haoran for what they perceive to be his resolve to return to nature and not crave the recognition and rewards of officialdom. Some have suggested that Meng Haoran's reputation grew out of his contemporaries' love for his person and the bias in his favor in post-Tang poetry collections. I find those kinds of comments somewhat demeaning, as if Meng's reputation, especially when he is paired with Wang Wei, is undeserved. There is a spontaneity in Meng's poems that is both personable and liberating, and not only when he was inebriated. On the other hand, the perception of his wisdom or loftiness, then and now, may be somewhat exaggerated, as I find quite a bit of regret and frustration in the poems, more pronounced in the earlier poems, but not entirely absent even in the later ones. Compared to Wang Wei, the latter's poetry is certainly more serene, but then again, Wang Wei lived a relatively leisurely life. Nevertheless, the egoless self that is often remarked upon in their poetry I find even more convincing in Meng than in Wang. Wang's disappearing act is artful, but Meng's absence of ego is more natural, in that he remains in his poems without exerting any pressure on us to pay attention to him and his non-ego. Reading his poetry is like being with a friend who is non-competitive, non-judgmental, and non-contriving.

Wang Wei was almost the same age as Li Bai, although they never met nor sought each other out, let alone become friends. That two poets as different as Li Bai and Wang Wei both admired and enjoyed many years of friendship with Meng Haoran goes to show what a personable man Meng was. When Meng went to the capital, Wang tried for several years to introduce the older man to his influential friends. By that time, Meng was already well-known among poets but was unsuccessful in his bid for a government post, in fact, he even failed that capricious *jinshi* exam. This next poem was written at Lake Dongting, China's second largest freshwater lake and a scenic spot, and presented to a Chancellor Zhang, almost as a sort of job application.

The opening of a poem is supposed to set a scene. Whether it

MY CHINA IN TANG POETRY

is successfully supported by the rest of the poem is one way to judge its success. This poem has been praised for amply fulfilling that requirement. The lake's abundance in this case sets the scene for Meng's reference to the overflowing wealth of the Tang dynasty, a time when, theoretically, talents were appreciated, and all good men wished to serve their emperor, or so they were taught. Remember, we are now at the historical arc called High Tang, the brightest spot in the Tang dynasty, when Li Bai was a young man, and Du Fu was just a baby. Meng, too, wanted to be of service to the emperor. The "raft" he was looking for in the poem is a patron who can recommend him. The "life of a recluse" was not chosen by him but chosen for him at this time, as he "failed" to cross the lake and join the productive "fishermen" on the other side.

GAZING ON LAKE DONGTING
PRESENTED TO CHANCELLOR ZHANG

An eighth month moon floats on flooded Lake Dongting:
A clear sky mirrored in its water; water merged with sky.
North Pool spills into South, surging waves thrashing shores,
shaking steamy vapors to envelop thriving Yue Yang City.
I have failed in my search for a raft to ferry me across.
Living this life of a recluse, I have let my emperor down.
Watching the fishermen across the shore ply their trade,
I can only sigh and admire the abundance of their catch.

FLOATING ON CLOUDS

望洞庭湖贈張丞相

八月湖水平，
涵虛混太清。
氣蒸雲夢澤，
波撼岳陽城。
欲濟無舟楫，
端居恥聖明。
坐觀垂釣者，
空有羨魚情。

During this time of patron-hunting and trips to the capital, Meng was still relatively young and naturally worried about his future. This next poem might have been written on his way to Chang'an. The boatman is treated like a fortune-teller here. The Huai is Huai River, close to Chang'an, the capital. Waves describe the turmoil he can expect to find there.

THE BOATMAN'S ANSWER

As the sun was setting, I asked the boatman,
"How much longer will it take to arrive?"
"There's a bay coming up, a good place to moor.
Further towards the Huai, waves will be high."

問舟子

向夕問舟子，
前程復幾多？
灣頭正好泊，
淮裏足風波。

MY CHINA IN TANG POETRY

OVERNIGHT BY RIVER JIANDE

I rowed my boat into the misty shallows
as sunlight recedes. New worries arise.
Fierce and empty, the sky reflects the wilderness,
as translucent water pulls the moon closer to me.

宿建德江

移舟泊煙渚，
日暮客愁新。
野曠天低樹，
江清月近人。

Meng Haoran, like Li Bai, was a traveler, though his travels were not quite as dramatic or as dramatically described as Li's. They are usually around the Xiangyang area where his farm was located. The region itself is a picturesque area with many interesting places to visit. These travels sometimes fulfilled a purpose, like visiting old friends or seeking out possible opportunities, but often they were purely for sightseeing, or visiting with Buddhist and Daoist monks. The next poem takes us to Phoenix Forest Range, 鳳林山, Fenglin shan, where there is a temple. This is three miles southeast of Xiangyang, where Meng lived, and where he would eventually be buried.

FLOATING ON CLOUDS

VISITING THE WESTERN RANGE
OF PHOENIX FOREST SHRINE

While we are still young and strong, we have come
to enjoy ourselves among these rocks and waterways.
The misty vista from up here opens onto distant treetops,
colors of spring spread silently, taking over hilly slopes.
Friends get along much better with a jug of wine to share,
and someone's brought a qin to strum out a few wild songs.
Let's not worry about getting lost on returning in the dark,
we'll hail the moon and ask her to show us the way home.

遊鳳林寺西嶺

共喜年華好，
來游水石間。
煙容開遠樹，
春色滿幽山。
壺酒朋情洽，
琴歌野興閒。
莫愁歸路暝，
招月伴人還。

　　Wuling 武陵 is where Tao Qian had set his imaginary Peach Blossom Village where immortals live, an idyllic place which, once one leaves it, one will not be able to find again. Wuling is near present-day Changde, in Hunan, west of Lake Dongting. A narrative poem by Wang Wei set in the same place will be found in the next chapter.

MY CHINA IN TANG POETRY

BOATING ON WULING RIVER

River pathways in Wuling are narrow,
once boats enter the blossoming forest,
it is hard to find one's way out or in again, no one
knows where Tao's immortal village can be found.
As we wind through the blue water, it closes up on us.
As clouds disappear, the green canopy grows shadier still,
until all one hears is the call of gibbons, shrill yet relaxing,
clearing away any impurity one might harbor in one's heart.

武陵泛舟

武陵川路狹，
前棹入花林。
莫測幽源里，
仙家信幾深。
水回青嶂合，
雲度綠溪陰。
坐聽閒猿嘯，
彌清塵外心。

The next poem, "Early Plums" is a different sort of poem and seems uncharacteristic of Meng. Like the observer in the Lake Dongting poem, he is someone looking in from the outside.

FLOATING ON CLOUDS

EARLY PLUMS

Early plum buds have started to blossom in the park.
As usual, they are the first to brave the still cold weather.
Young women reach for the best branches, bending them
to tear off and take home for vases on their dressers.
Not satisfied with nature's creation, they need to cut
and tailor the flowers to what looks best in their eyes.

早梅

園中有早梅,
年例犯寒開。
少婦曾攀折,
將歸插鏡台。
猶言看不足,
更欲剪刀裁。

I placed "Early Plums" here because it feels like a Chang'an sort of poem, somewhat out of character for Meng, as he seems to be critical of the young ladies, though on the surface it is a light-hearted sort of poem. Maybe being in Chang'an made him meaner. Still, in my impression of him, this is as mean as he gets. Competition and possession were the ways of the capital. Even from the few poems we have seen from Meng Haoran, this was not the way he wanted to live. In this way, he was more like Wang Wei than he was like Li Bai. Much as Li Bai was able to immerse himself in nature when he was in nature, he was still indignant at the powers that be for not appreciating his immense talent. Meng never seemed angry even at his most frustrated. After failing the unpredictable imperial exam, he had at first wanted to petition the emperor and make his case, but this was not an easy task, and he would need to find someone in power to get him in. Before long, he was ready to give up and go home. Chu is just another way to refer to the seat of power, and the Xiang River runs by his home in Xiangyang.

WINTER CAME EARLY BRINGING THOUGHTS OF HOME BY THE RIVER

Leaves falling, wild geese flying south, and
the north wind has brought a chill to the river.
My home is in the crook of the Xiang River,
far from these mountainous clouds of Chu.
My homesick tears are drained away, as I watch
that lonely sail disappear on the distant horizon.
Which way can one go in a sea of confusion?
The sunset spreads slowly, taking over the water.

早寒江上思歸

木落雁南度,
北風江上寒。
我家襄水曲,
遙隔楚雲端。
鄉淚客中盡,
孤帆天際看。
迷津欲有問,
平海夕漫漫。

FLOATING ON CLOUDS

SAYING GOODBYE TO WANG WEI

What is this do-nothing here waiting for?
Every day he comes home empty-handed.
Follow the hermits into the wilderness, I say,
but I couldn't bear to leave my dear friends.
Since no one in power would lend a hand,
and rarely can one's voice be heard, perhaps
the best way forward is solitary seclusion:
go back to my old garden and shut the door.

留別王維

寂寂竟何待，
朝朝空自歸。
欲尋芳草去，
惜與故人違。
當路誰相假，
知音世所稀。
只應守寂寞，
還掩故園扉。

In fact, to say he was never given a chance to enter officialdom is probably incorrect, and unfair to Wang Wei, as his friend did try to help him. Then, there are stories here and there even after he left the capital, about people admiring his abilities and wanting to lend him a hand, even offering him appointments, but he would either refuse or deliberately arrive late or leave a post soon after arriving. Perhaps he was just not cut out to be a court official. Maybe this was what Li Bai meant about him. And perhaps not fitting in was a bit of a badge of honor, not that I am downplaying the unfairness of the system.

MY CHINA IN TANG POETRY

By way of introducing Wang Wei and to show how well he knew his friend, let me insert a poem Wang wrote, most likely in answer to the above Meng poem upon his leaving Chang'an.

FAREWELL MY FRIEND, by Wang Wei

Here is where we say goodbye. I dismount and drink
to your health, asking, "And where are you headed now?"
You bow your head and say, "Nothing's going my way,
I may as well go home to South Mountain's embrace."
"It's time to put an end to the endless questions," I say,
"follow the floating clouds to where time knows no end."

送別，王維

下馬飲君酒，
問君何所之.
君言不得意,
歸臥南山垂.
但去莫復問,
白雲無盡時.

The next poem would have been written soon after his return to Xiangyang, but, if the story below is to be believed, he would have written it in anticipation of retiring.

RETURNING TO SOUTH MOUNTAIN AT YEAR'S END

No longer petitioning at the Imperial Gate,
I have returned to my hut at South Mountain.
Lacking talent, I have not been chosen to serve,
and I'm often sick, few friends come round anymore.

FLOATING ON CLOUDS

My white hair reminds me every day I am getting old.
A new spring has come to chase away another year.
Worries and regrets have replaced sound sleep.
Pines block the moon from my window.

歲暮歸南山

北闕休上書，
南山歸敝廬。
不才明主棄，
多病故人疏。
白髮催年老，
青陽逼歲除。
永懷愁不寐，
松月夜窗虛。

The anecdote associated with this poem would have been amusing if it were not so pathetic. According to this story, Meng was visiting Wang Wei when Emperor Xuanzong also happened to visit unannounced. Meng was so scared he hid under his friend's bed and even wet his pants. One is not to meet the emperor or look at his face directly unless summoned and given permission. When the emperor heard that Meng was there, he honored the poet by calling to him and asking for a poem. Unfortunately, perhaps out of nervousness, Meng recited the above poem, which annoyed Xuanzong, with the half-line, "I have not been chosen to serve," as if the all-important man did not have the wisdom to recognize his talent. "When have I not chosen you?" The emperor asked and dismissed him. Wang Wei said to Meng later that he should have recited the Lake Dongting poem instead as it was more pleasing, but now he had blown his chances forever. True or not, Meng never made it into court.

MY CHINA IN TANG POETRY

Experiences at the capital were not all dread and disappointments. Given his personality, he made many friends. The following is a poem written about a party he attended. This Zhang is most likely the same one to whom he addressed that earlier poem at Lake Dongting. Cold Stove Day is a winter festival when one does not cook; it is sometimes translated as Cold Food Day. "A good snow". 瑞雪, is timely snow, dubbed by farmers as auspicious, because it warms up the environment and kills undesirable insects, plus it is a frozen reservoir for use when it melts. This kind of snowfall foretells a good harvest. Poetry contests refer to the drinking game of poetry-making. A candle is marked and used as a stopwatch, usually about an inch of candle for a poem — that is, before the candle burns to the marked spot, you have to complete the poem assigned. If you fail, you have to drink up. And finally, superior wine is supposed to not confuse the mind or make one drunk. Meng Haoran is describing a sort of perfect party here. An alternate text gives the last two lines as: "Feeling woozy, I lay down and fell asleep. / Before I knew it, cockcrow woke me." 醉來方欲臥，不覺曉雞鳴。

COLD STOVE BANQUET AT ZHANG MINGFU's MANSION

Sign of a good year this timely snow, a whole foot
has fallen within the first half of the first night watch.
You've arranged seating for our drinking companions,
and marked a candle for the poetry contest as we drink.
The room is pleasantly warmed by pots of incense,
and the string player's strokes so delicate and pure
are the perfect accompaniment for this superior wine,
clearing the mind. Dawn rises to welcome me home.

寒夜張明府宅宴

瑞雪初盈尺，
寒宵始半更。
列筵邀酒伴，
刻燭限詩成。
香炭金爐暖，
嬌弦玉指清。
厭厭不覺醉，
歸路曉霞生。

On his way back to Xiangyang, he took the opportunity to do a bit of sightseeing. In this poem we see the childlike Meng, chatty and eager to get to his destination. Yuezhong 越中, mentioned in the poem, is the coastal area that Li Bai loved so much.

CHATTING WITH MY BOATMATES AS WE CROSS JIEJIANG

On the calm water after low tide, before the wind rises,
we share this small boat sailing together to the other shore.
Every so often I stretch my neck to look towards sky's end,
asking, "which of those green mountains is Yuezhong?"

渡浙江問舟中人

潮落江平未有風，
扁舟共濟與君同。
時時引領望天末，
何處青山是越中。

MY CHINA IN TANG POETRY

Chinese people like to address others by their birth order, especially close friends or family friends. Whoever this Mr. Liu was in the next poem, he was the big brother in his own family, and his good friends would call him big brother as well. Double Ninth is the Ninth Day of the Ninth lunar month. It is a festival called Chong Yang when people like to go to a high place, usually a mountain or hilly spot, to picnic.

The festival originated with a legend about escaping calamity. The following poem may have been written around the same time or on another occasion, but it is in the same vein as the previous sightseeing poem.

SENT TO BIG BROTHER LIU
ON DOUBLE NINTH FROM DRAGON BAY

> Dragon Bay is just north of Yuzhang.
> Sailing past on Double Ninth, I stopped
> to see how they celebrate this festival day.
> Such rousing scenery of hills and lakes.
> Might someone share his wine with me?
> A few drinks later, we started to sing and
> rowed till the sun sank low into the water,
> and I drifted away with the evening waves.

FLOATING ON CLOUDS

九日龍沙寄劉大

龍沙豫章北,
九日掛帆過。
風俗因時見,
湖山發興多。
客中誰送酒?
棹裏自成歌。
歌竟乘流去,
滔滔任夕波。

The following three farewell poems are some examples of Meng's empathetic nature. Everyone in these next poems are fellow scholars pretty much suffering the same unpredictable fate as himself. The first two here are, at the moment, fortunate, and seemed to be heading for a bright future. The last example is about one who was down on his luck at the time. The Minister Zhang in the next poem is not the one to whom the Dongting Lake poem was addressed; Zhang 張 is another pretty common last name. Vermillion door in the second line refers to the red doors indicating the residences of officials at the capital. As noted in Li Bai's story in *Superstars*, hierarchies are color-coded in the Tang dynasty down to the clothes people are allowed to wear.

SENDING OFF MINISTER ZHANG TO THE CAPITAL

On this gleaming water we have often sailed together.
Unexpectedly, you are summoned to a vermillion door.
I am happy for you but already feeling my loss and
missing the beautiful, clear voices of you and your qin.

MY CHINA IN TANG POETRY

送張郎中遷京

碧溪常共賞，
朱邸忽遷榮。
豫有相思意，
聞君琴上聲。

Since the emperor is called the Son of Heaven, in decorations of the throne and his robes we often find blue clouds. Thus, the opening line to the next poem.

SEEING OFF A FRIEND HEADING FOR THE CAPITAL

You rode a blue cloud, higher and higher, towards heaven.
Now I gaze on the far green peaks, watching for your return.
These peaks will not see that cloud you have gone off on,
my recluse robe is soaked through with tears of farewell.

送友人之京

君登青雲去，
予望青山歸。
雲山從此別，
淚濕薜羅衣。

His question in the next poem reminds me of friends who come from the north to the south of the United States and, finding that the trees are not as tall in the warmer region, feel homesick for them. Jiangling is in the south of China. Flora and fauna are such big parts of our attachment to places, especially homes, consciously or subconsciously, no wonder Confucius thought them so important; and since all knowledge feeds into making the country a better place, knowing one's plants has much to do with good government. Does this mean even though the capital, the place of governance, is so remote from where most people live, those who govern must remain connected to the people on the ground? To what affects their lives? It seems to me Meng's little poems to his minister friends are much more than the sentimental goodbyes they at first appear to be.

JUST MISSED MINISTER YUAN AT LUOZHONG

I came to Luoyang to visit the talented Minister Yuan
only to hear that he has already been exiled to Jiangling.
I hear plum blossoms come early over there,
can they compare to the spring flowers here?

洛中訪袁拾遺不遇

洛陽訪才子,
江嶺作流人。
聞說梅花早,
何如北地春。

There were also quite a number of Daoist and Buddhist monks that Meng liked to drop in on once in a while to study, meditate, and discuss the scriptures. Master Rong, in the next two poems was one of them. The first one is one of those poems about visiting someone and not finding them home, which happens so often we might call it a genre or trope. Depending on one's reaction to the disappointment, the poem takes on philosophical significance. In this poem, Meng was not upset when he couldn't find the monk. (The opening line with the monk's indoor garment, his robe, hanging on a hook, indicated that he had gone out.) Since

MY CHINA IN TANG POETRY

the serenity outside the sanctuary was just as pleasing to him (second line), he spent all day enjoying the quiet (third line) and lingered (last line) to soak up the last peaceful drops of the day on his way home. If he had come to talk to the monk, hoping to be enlightened, the monk's absence may have given him an even better appreciation of Buddhist/Daoist teachings.

DROPPING BY MASTER RONG'S SANCTUARY

> The sanctuary was empty but for a monk's robe hanging on a hook.
> No one's been here, just a few birds flying above the burbling stream.
> By the time I was halfway down the slope the sun was already setting.
> I halted to listen to temple bells ringing through the layers of greenery.

過融上人蘭若

山頭禪室挂僧衣，
窓外無人溪鳥飛，
黃昏半在下山路，
却聽泉聲戀翠微。

Time elapsed between his last visit to Master Rong and this next poem, and a new retreat was built, or at least the old one was renovated. I have added the word "Buddha" to the "gold" in the opening line for English readers and even Chinese who are not familiar with Buddhist color symbolism. In Buddhism, gold represents the sun, the source of life and enlightenment. That is why you see so much gold in Buddhist temples and monasteries.

To the less ethereal, gold also means happiness and other forms of wealth.

POEM FOR MASTER RONG'S MOUNTAIN RETREAT

It's a new retreat, built in Buddha's gold:
stone steps wrapped in a ring of living spring.
On your mat you sit, in the mist of lotus scent,
under great pines and cypress trees, incense lit.
Rain comes as you meditate, and flies off at dawn,
scattering petals from the heavens to bless the earth.
Trying to fathom the mysteries, time passed by. So much
to pursue as the sun sets and my horse wants to go home.

題融公蘭若

精舍買金開，
流泉遶砌迴，
芰荷薰講席，
松柏映香臺。
法雨晴飛去，
天花晝下來。
談玄殊未已，
歸騎夕陽催。

The old friend in the next poem must have been a fellow Daoist, as his not being home meant one thing to Meng: he was off to the mountains collecting herbs to make elixirs in his cave, like Pang De in the Master Rong poems coming up. Two stories are alluded to in the poem. The story behind the dragon bamboos in the opening line is that of Fei Changfang, a Daoist turned immortal. Fei rode home on a stalk of bamboo which turned into a dragon when he threw it away. Then, there is the story of Liu Bei, who is believed to be the legitimate heir to Han in the Three Kingdoms Period. Apparently, this was the spot by the river where, being chased by enemy soldiers, he was almost caught, when his horse made an unimaginable thirty-foot leap across the river and saved his life. In other words, there is something supernatural at work where Meng's friend lived. The mention of garden and field means that, like Tao Qian, this friend is a recluse and maybe a poet as well.

LOOKING UP AN OLD FRIEND AT SANDALWOOD BROOK

Surrounded by flowers and magical dragon bamboos,
this is where Liu Bei's horse made his fantastic jump.
Since I cannot find you in your garden or your field,
I expect you have gone off to a cave in the mountains.

檀溪尋故人

花伴成龍竹，
池分躍馬溪。
田園人不見，
疑向洞中棲。

The next few poems give a feel for his life at the family farm situated near South Mountain. We call him a recluse, but generally, by "recluse" we simply mean someone who was not in officialdom and not really a hermit or an ascetic. Even the bona fide hermits these poets admired, like the famous Late Eastern Han recluse Pang De 龐德, had a wife and children and many friends, including Zhuge Liang, the great strategist from

FLOATING ON CLOUDS

Romance of the Three Kingdoms. Pang De is found in quite a few of Meng's poems. (Here's an interesting aside: Ezra Pound's name in Chinese is Pang De (for Poun-de), using the same characters as the historical Pang De, who was a military general before he "hid". I wonder if Pound chose this transliteration himself or if somebody else gave him that name.) Deer Gate is where Pang De built his "thatch hut" and made his herbal concoctions in a cave nearby. This place is near Meng's farm and he, too, like a fan, built his "thatch hut" there.

ON MY WAY HOME TO DEER GATE, AN EVENING SONG

>A distant mountain shrine tolls out the evening hour.
>At the fishermen's dock, a noisy crowd has gathered.
>They follow the sandy paths home to their villages,
>while I board the ferry and head back to Deer Gate.
>A bright moon combs through the dark, misty woods,
>lights up the old stone hut where Pang De once lived
>at the end of a long pathway through the pine forest.
>Only a recluse would be coming home to a place like this.

>夜歸鹿門山歌

>山寺鐘鳴晝已昏，
>漁梁渡頭爭渡喧。
>人隨沙岸向江村，
>余亦乘舟歸鹿門。
>鹿門月照開煙樹，
>忽到龐公棲隱處。
>巖扉松徑長寂寥，
>惟有幽人自來去。

MY CHINA IN TANG POETRY

Meng the recluse is forever the amateur, and that is what is so endearing about him. He is always down to earth and connected to others. There are a few poems we know of where we find this Abbot Mei in the next poem. *Mei*, means plums or plum blossoms. I don't think the abbot's name has much to do with Meng's love of the flower, but it is an amusing coincidence, and as you shall see, there are a couple of anecdotes associated with Meng and the plum flower. First, a few notes for understanding the next poem. The Queen Mother of the West, an important Daoist deity, uses bluebirds as messengers (third line.) "Golden stove" refers to the earthen pots Daoists used to make elixirs and other such concoctions (line five.) "Immortal peaches" refer to the peaches that are supposed to be found in paradise and confer immortality and are eaten by gods (line six.) "Rainbow Brew" is the special wine that is drunk by immortals and supposed to confer upon drinkers their "baby faces" or "youthful look" (line seven.) All this talk of immortality is simply used to color the experience and tell us how enlightening and enjoyable it was for him. Now that we know that Qing Ming is a festival for remembering the dead, this feast on this particular occasion becomes doubly memorable.

INVITED BY DAOIST ABBOT MEI FOR A QING MING FEAST

Resting in the forest, I was fretting the end of spring,
soaking up the last of the many splendors of nature,
when suddenly a bluebird messenger appeared before me,
with an invitation to come to Abbot Mei's Red Pine Lodge.
Stepping in, I see that his golden stove has just been lit,
and immortal peaches are in full blossom in the garden.
If his Rainbow Brew can indeed confer youth upon me,
I'm sure he won't stint his wine, and I sure won't be shy.

FLOATING ON CLOUDS

清明日宴梅道士房

林臥愁春盡,
搴帷覽物華。
忽逢青鳥使,
邀入赤松家。
金灶初開火,
仙桃正發花。
童顏若可駐,
何惜醉流霞。

Friendship is a major theme in Chinese poetry and is central to Meng's life. Friendship, drinking, and poetry, one might say triumph over love and marriage. Come to think of it, even though filial piety tops the list of values in Chinese society, this Confucian value does not appear as often as one would have expected in Tang poems, not even in those of this filial son.

Brothers are missed, children not as much, it seems. Meng had a wife at some point, as filial sons are expected to marry and have children. Meng seemed to have produced two, but mostly, friends, neighbors, farmers, hermits, and other poets and scholar officials, populate his poems.

MY CHINA IN TANG POETRY

FOR ZHANG, MY COUNTRY NEIGHBOR, AN INSCRIPTION

My farmhouse happens to be next to yours,
and we both appreciate the same things in life:
farming and fishing are our leisurely activities,
and you will not find our wine jugs ever empty.
The vulgar will not be welcomed at our doors,
we only invite immortals, human or ghost, and
we're not interested in so-called, "virtuous men."
If they are Pang De admirers, they are our guests.

題張野人園廬

與君園廬並，
微尚頗亦同。
耕釣方自逸，
壺觴趣不空。
門無俗士駕，
人有上皇風。
何必先賢傳，
惟稱龐德公。

    This next poem, "Visiting an Old Friend's Farm", makes use of two *chengyus* 成语 (set phrases) which came from ancient stories. The first one is "preparing chicken and millet" *ju ji shu*, 具雞黍, which goes back to the legend of two friends who enjoyed each other's company so much that they would travel many miles to visit each other, at which time they would prepare a nice dinner (chicken and millet) with good wine. Preparing nice dinners for friends has thus come to be called "preparing chicken and millet". The other *chengyu* is "discussing mulberry and jute," *hua sang ma,* 話桑麻, which I have translated into "talk farm talk," because that is what the phrase means. Why mulberry and jute? Because mulberry leaves feed silkworms and, therefore, trees are grown for silk, and jute is used for making coarse clothes and sacks, for utilitarian farming purposes. At the end of the poem, the chrysanthemums bridge the ideas of farming and reclusion, in that growing chrysanthemums to sell is a farming concern, and these flowers bring Tao Qian to mind as well. Again, Chong Yang is the Double Ninth, and the practice of going up to a high place originated with a story about escaping from danger, thus hiding, like a recluse. Both farming and reclusion are, of course, Tao Qian activities.

VISITING AN OLD FRIEND'S FARM

My old friend prepared chicken and millet
and invited me to his farmhouse for dinner.
Tall green trees encircle his pleasant village,
blue hills wrapping around the village wall.
Outside his window are fields of vegetation,
inside, we chat and drink and talk farm talk.
I'll come again when Chong Yang rolls round,
and see how your chrysanthemums are doing.

MY CHINA IN TANG POETRY

過故人莊

故人具雞黍，
邀我至田家。
綠樹村邊合，
青山郭外斜。
開筵面場圃，
把酒話桑麻。
待到重陽日，
還來就菊花。

THOUGHTS ON AN AUTUMN MOONLIT NIGHT

In the autumn sky the moon hangs there all by itself.
Down here, dewdrops glisten in radiant rainbow hues.
Magpies, startled from their nests, unable to settle down,
fireflies, in the half-light, fly in under my open screen.
Through the sparse branches of winter shrubberies
comes the sound of neighbors' pestles pounding spice.
The date of your return seems ever more remote. I strain
to look into the darkness but see no sign of your arrival.

秋宵月下有懷

秋空明月懸，
光彩露霑濕。
驚鵲棲未定，
飛螢捲簾入。
庭槐寒影疏，
鄰杵夜聲急。
佳期曠何許，
望望空佇立。

The sound of pounding pestles here is Meng giving a twist to the cliché of the sound of laundry paddles used for clothes washing, usually at a stream, that is used often in poems to evoke longing for an absent family member, usually a husband or lover. Here the dinner preparations at his neighbors' houses remind him of making dinner with or for his friend.

"Old Xin" in the next poem appears several times in Meng's poetry. In this one he has either died or gone away from Meng's neighborhood.

SUMMER AT SOUTHERN PAVILION, THINKING OF DEAR OLD XIN

Suddenly gone, the sunlight from the western hills.
In the east, the moon gradually rises on the pond.
I untie my hair, enjoying this evening's coolness,
open the window and lie down on my spacious bed.
A gentle breeze brings in lotus scent. In the silence,
I even hear dew drops dripping from bamboo stalks.
I thought to get my qin and sing along with its music,
but there's no one to enjoy it with now that you are gone.
These thoughts remind me of how I have missed you.
In dreams tonight, you will keep me troubled company.

MY CHINA IN TANG POETRY

夏日南亭懷辛大

山光忽西落，
池月漸東上。
散髮乘夕涼，
開軒臥閒敞。
荷風送香氣，
竹露滴清響。
欲取鳴琴彈，
恨無知音賞。
感此懷故人，
中宵勞夢想。

As we have seen earlier, even at home in Xiangyang, there are many places to visit. The next poem was written at Xian Shan, or Mount Xian, not far from his farm. Yuliang Island and vicinity is a beautiful area then and now. Before the Han Dynasty, Xiangyang was collectively called Yuliangzhou. It is a peninsula surrounded by water on three sides and mountains on one. It has been a tourist destination for a long, long time. Yang Hu (221-278), mentioned at the end of the poem, was a famous general and strategist of the Jin dynasty. He was stationed at the military post on this Mount Xian and treated the people well. Upon his death the locals built this monument in remembrance of his kindness and called it the "Monument of Tears", because it was his plan that was used to conquer Eastern Wu, but he did not live to see it come to fruition.

FLOATING ON CLOUDS

ON VISITING MOUNT XIAN WITH A FEW FRIENDS

Lives are ever-changing, growth follows decay,
events come and go and become history today.
On this hallowed ground we find ourselves
treading on the footprints our ancestors made.
Yuliang waters so clear and shallow, rocks float.
Leaves fall on clouds on chilly Dream Cloud Lake.
On this stone slab we find Yang Hu's life story.
I am left in tears on reading it; my clothes, soaked.

與諸子登峴山

人事有代謝，
往來成古今。
江山留勝跡，
我輩復登臨。
水落魚梁淺，
天寒夢澤深。
羊公碑尚在，
讀罷淚沾襟。

Incidentally, Meng Haoran was also called Meng Xiangyang by the people of Xiangyang who loved him. A giant stone statue of him is carved into this mountain and was unveiled in 2019; on the mountain wall is carved the poem "Spring Dawn", with which we began this chapter.

Let's end this short selection with his favorite flower, the two famous plum blossom anecdotes that people tell about him. One is from the early part of his life and other, the latter. In both, we witness the childlike enthusiasm, curiosity and wonder that is Meng Haoran.

MY CHINA IN TANG POETRY

An Anecdote About the Younger Meng

Wang Wei had made a name for himself in both art and poetry from an early age. We're not sure how it began, but Meng Haoran and he had been corresponding with each other even before Meng ventured out of Xiangyang to the capital. One year, during that early period, Wang Wei announced that he was coming to Xiangyang to visit, and Meng was so excited that he got together as many of the artists and poets that he knew in the area and prepared a great feast to welcome him, to help him "clean off the dust from traveling," as the Chinese say. Wine and maybe bream may have been involved. Beside feasting and drinking, poetry and music would have been shared. As host, Meng Haoran sang an opening couplet for the guest to complete. He may have spent days thinking about it beforehand, and proudly recited:

> Plum petals fall by the thousands, vying with the fluttering snow,
> bamboo shoots up three feet in two days, matching the heavy rain.

Wang Wei raised his cup and said:

> The rain-soaked forest delayed lighting of the village stoves.
> Simple meals hurriedly prepared for farmers out in the fields.

The lines were so apt, fitted so well with the Meng's invitation for him to harmonize with his opening couplet, bringing nature's gift and human warmth and the activities of local villagers to bear, that everyone applauded, and wanted the young master to share with them the secret of his genius. Wang Wei could not refuse and came up with the following advice:

> It is not how well you can manipulate the words at your disposal, but how well you are able to make your surroundings come alive.

This, according to storytellers of the anecdote, was such an inspiration to Meng that he began to truly study the natural beauty around him, which we eventually found in his poetry. Years later, he was to impress another gathering of literati at a Mid-Autumn Festival, where one of his couplets won much applause, so much so the poem never got finished!

> Tenuous clouds gently rippling River Han's surface.
> Misty raindrops barely skim the tops of wutong leaves.

An Anecdote About the Old Man

On the banks of the Han River all year round, rain or shine, winter, spring, summer, or fall, an old man is seen with his head down, as if looking for something in the sand, only occasionally looking up at the faraway peaks, before resuming his investigation.

One day, in the depth of winter, snow was falling like goose feathers, and the banks were covered in a thin carpet of white, and yet the old man was still there. By now people knew the old man was Meng Haoran, and that he had gone into reclusion at Deer Gate. Finally, a curious passerby who knew him went up to him and asked,

"Master Meng, it's so cold out here, why are you stomping on the snow? What are you looking for?"

"Ha, ha, ha," Meng looked up and said, "I am looking for plum blossoms, don't you know?"

The man looked down and saw that Meng's footprints had

made patterns that indeed looked like plum petals strewn on the ground. The story spread, and someone made a lighthearted verse about the incident:

> Heavy snow fell throughout the winter season,
> falling like goose feathers everywhere you go.
> Haoran is not bothered by bitter wind and ice,
> he's happily hunting plum flowers in the snow!

2

Wang Wei 王维 (699 – 761)
South Mountain Dreaming

Wang Wei was born in 699 to a family that had contributed thirteen prime ministers to the Tang dynasty. Given such a prestigious background, he was well-educated and groomed for great things. By fifteen, he was an accomplished poet, painter, and musician. In 717, he won first place in the *jinshi* exam, and two years later, was appointed Assistant to the Imperial Director of Music. By the time he died in 759, at age sixty, he had held positions at twelve departments in the ministries of war, justice, and works. He did marry, but his wife died when he was in his thirties without bearing any children. He never remarried and remained childless. After his mother died, twenty years later, he more or less withdrew from public life and lived in his country estate at Lantian, along the Wang River. It was during this time of reclusion that he remembered that couplet he came up with when he visited Meng Haoran in Xiangyang, or at least that is a plausible explanation for why we find the couplet that so impressed his audience then applied to an entirely different village in the opening couplet of the poem, "Web River Village After a Deluge," written years later. I shall explain why I am calling the Wang River the Web River later when we come to those poems. Chronologically, this poem should be placed with

MY CHINA IN TANG POETRY

Wang Wei's "retirement" poems at the end of this chapter, but I've put it here because we just came from Meng Haoran's story. There are two stories and one botanical fact that help us read this next poem. First, before we messed with it, each hibiscus flower bloom only for one day. (There are hybrids now that last longer.) Thus, Wang Wei meditating on the hibiscus means more than just watching a flower open. The last couplet alludes to two stories, one about seating and the other about gulls. The seating story is in Zhuangzi where the Daoist philosopher Yang Zhu 楊朱 (ca. 395-335) went to seek out the Daoist founder Laozi. On his way there, he passed by an inn where everyone gave him their seats when he walked in, being the obvious upper-class gentleman, but on his journey home, when he stopped at the same place, nobody bothered to get up. In other words, class and rank and such things no longer applied since, having been enlightened by the wise man himself, he was now a full-fledged Daoist. In other words, to the true Daoist, class and rank mean nothing. Now, for the story of the seagulls. This is a story from another ancient text, the fifth century BCE Liezi, 列子, where a man was at the seaside playing with the seagulls that were coming very close to him. One day, his father told him to go and catch some seagulls for him (for a dish?) When the man returned thereafter, the seagulls were suspicious of him and kept their distance.

FLOATING ON CLOUDS

WEB RIVER VILLAGE AFTER A DELUGE

The rain-soaked forest delayed the lighting of village stoves.
Simple meals are hurriedly prepared for farmers out in the
    fields.
I see egrets cross the borderless sky on newly flooded paddies,
and hear oriole songs break through summer's dense green
    forest.
Sitting in contemplation, I watch the hibiscus bloom and die,
under the tall pine trees, I enjoy my monk's tea and okra meal.
Peasants no longer need to give this old man their seats,
and there is no need for seagulls to keep their distance.

積雨輞川莊

積雨空林煙火遲，
蒸藜炊黍餉東菑。
漠漠水田飛白鷺，
陰陰夏木囀黃鸝。
山中習靜觀朝槿，
松下清齋折露葵。
野老與人爭席罷，
海鷗何事更相疑。

Since the 1960's, many American poets have been attracted by the Zen quality of some Chinese poetry, and Wang Wei is at the top of the list of poets that have been imitated and translated. Zen Buddhism as we call it in the west is derived from Chan Buddhism. Zen is the Japanese pronunciation of the Chinese word, *chan* 禪, and written with the same character. Wang Wei was a practicing Buddhist and wealthy enough to have country estates, where he could go and distance himself from the mess

MY CHINA IN TANG POETRY

that is everyday living. I shall begin this introduction with two such poems, "Bird Call Valley" and "A Painting". They are both *juejus*.

They also exemplify that ability Wang Wei has to disappear into the scene of a poem and leave one contemplating. "Bird Call Valley" is often cited as an example of this disappearing act. Chronologically, this is a later poem, probably written around the time of the "Web River Valley" series. This poem was set in his friend Wang Pu's estate nearby. The poem is a five-character *jueju*, that is, a twenty-word quatrain. The Chinese word in the title after "Bird Call" is 澗 *jian*, meaning a stream or gulley that runs between two mountains. Thus, I am calling it a valley. I have, on two different days, come up with two English renditions of the Chinese verse. On first encounter you might find them quite different. Let me explain with a line-by-line reading, but first, a trot or word-for-word translation:

人	閒	桂	花	落
person people, I,	at ease leisurely, few	cassia(s)	flower(s)	fall
夜	靜	春	山	空
night evening	silent, quiet	spring	mountain	empty
月	出	驚	山	鳥
moon	rise(s)	frighten, startle	mountain	bird(s) come(s) out
時	鳴	春	澗	中
occasional, occasionally	call(s)	spring	stream	in, inside, among

FLOATING ON CLOUDS

As you can see from this trot, there is no indication in classical Chinese as to singular or plural nouns, nor do adjectives and verbs give that information. One is guided only by context and choice. Call it freeing or ambiguous. In this case, the first word is usually read as "person or people". It is, however, sometimes used to refer to oneself, especially in context. Here, together with the second word, "at ease", it reads, "I am at ease" or "the leisurely me." Read this way, the first line means, "At ease, I (idly walk) (while) cassia flowers fall (around me.)" On the other hand, the first two words can also mean "people" and "few". This would give us a first line that reads: "(There are) few people around and cassias are falling."

The second line gives us: "On this quiet night, the spring mountain is empty," or, "The night is quiet, it is spring, and no one is about in this mountain scene." We feel that there is a causal relationship between the silence and the scene because there seems to be a causal relationship between the person and the flowers in the first line. These couple of relationships are implied also because parallel structure in couplets is the norm in the *jueju*. Lines one and two and lines three and four make two pairs of parallel structured lines.

In the third line, the verb, "frighten or startle" stands out almost violently, disturbing this quiet scene not with a noise, but the suggestion of a noise or movement vis-à-vis the moon, which brings about the movement or noise of the birds. If there is an "I" in the first line, it will read, "I, too, am startled by the quiet moon rising". If we read it as just the scene with no one in it, then we see the sparsely populated scene suddenly lit up. The closing line brings all the "actions", such as they are, together, and if one were startled (just a bit) in the third line, one is returned to the harmonious scene of spring (flowing stream + mountain flowers in bloom), mountain stream (burbling noise + bird call),

MY CHINA IN TANG POETRY

and man/poet/a few people (not disturbing) the scene (being part of it, or at least simply observing it). This is what one calls "being at one with nature", a phrase I often mocked when I was not interested in, nor did I understand the state of, being "at one" with anything in my youth.

BIRD CALL VALLEY
(Two Versions)

Lazy days watching cassias fall.
Quiet nights in the springtime, hills empty.
Moonrise startles mountain birds.
Sporadic bird calls with burbling streams.

———∾———

Few people come. Cassias fall in silence.
Nighttime in the mountain in spring:
silence is broken as the moon appears,
startling birds, echoing water's flow.

鳥鳴澗

人閒桂花落，
夜靜春山空。
月出驚山鳥，
時鳴春澗中。

This is one of those rare instances where, even in English, one need not use a pronoun, and the "I" (poet or reader) can insert itself without being invited. As perfect as this *jueju* is, I must, as a responsible translator of this poem, reluctantly point out one mistake he made. I am speaking of the inconvenient matter of whether Wang Wei mistook some other flower for cassias, since this little yellow flower blooms in the fall and the poem is set in the spring. For those readers who cannot believe that such a great poet as Wang Wei could make this kind of a mistake, since, as you know, knowledge of flora and fauna is a Confucian scholar's prerequisite, two explanations have generally been given. One is that this is the kind of cassia that blooms twice a year, rare though it is, and two, this "mistake" is acceptable as poetic license. Some have even excused the poet/painter by asserting that there is a painting by Wang Wei where he had placed green banana leaves in a snow scene, perhaps deliberately, difficult as it would be to explain why. Since translators must make sense of a poem before they can translate, I have chosen the first explanation and allowed Wang's cassias to be the kind that blooms twice a year. Or he simply made a mistake!

There is a technique used in these poems that is also something of which Wang Wei is the acknowledged master. The technique is using sound to depict silence. All the quiet noises in these poems serve to accentuate the silence of the scene. "A Painting," cleverly illustrates the oft-cited brilliance of Wang's art, that "there is painting in his poetry and poetry in his painting".

A PAINTING

Gazing upon the far colors of the mountains,
listening to the noiseless flowing stream, I see
these flowers are in bloom though spring is over.
Birds are not startled by my coming onto the scene.

MY CHINA IN TANG POETRY

畫

遠看山有色，
近聽水無聲。
春去花還在，
人來鳥不驚。

Here are two more Wang Wei *juejus*. These two are set among lives of men and women. The second one might even be a love poem, as red berries (more accurately, red beans) are for lovers. They are actually both poems of longing, one for home and one for a special person. Even Wang Wei could not live on bird calls alone.

A MISCELLANEOUS POEM

Since you've just come from my village,
you must know what's new. Tell me,
has that plum tree in front of my window
started putting out its winter flowers?

雜詩

君自故鄉來，
應知故鄉事，
來日綺窗前，
寒梅著花未。

FLOATING ON CLOUDS

THINKING OF YOU

Down south is where red berries flourish
in spring, hanging in clumps on branches --
go and pick a few more sprigs this year and do
remember why they're called Thinking-of-You.

相思

紅豆生南國，
春來發幾枝？
願君多採摘，
此物最相思。

The following poem is a retelling of Tao Qian's "Peach Blossom Spring", another of the "stuff" that Tao's dreams are made on. One often comes across this idea of happening upon paradise on earth, getting lost and not finding it again. When you look for it, you can't find it, is an idea that can be applied to many things: love, meaning, and miscellaneous things. This is the poem I spoke of earlier when we were at Meng Haoran's Wuling. Just a reminder also, that the Qin dynasty came even before the Han.

PEACH BLOSSOM SPRING

The fisherman farther and farther upstream --
peach blossoms in season grew profusely on both banks.
So beautiful these trees and flowers, he lost track of time.
All the way down the stream there was no one in sight.
He walked straight into the woods and came to an entrance
to a cave, which suddenly opened out onto a different scene.

MY CHINA IN TANG POETRY

From afar it looked like a green and misty forest in the clouds,
but soon he found himself in a village full of bamboo and flowers.
The villagers said they had been there since the time of Han,
but their clothes suggested they could have been the people of Qin.
Wuling Spring has been their home for generations, and they have cultivated these fields and gardens. That night, the moon
came through the tall pines, casting a magic glow on the village.
Soon, it was dawn, and cocks were crowing amid barking dogs.
More people appeared from the houses to greet this stranger.
Everyone wanted to hear news about the outside world.
In the mornings, bright and early, the alleys were swept,
in the evenings, fishermen returned with their catch.
At first, they had come to escape the turmoil of the world.
As time went by, they became immortals and never returned.
From then on, they were content to live hidden in the mountains.
From the distance, mortals only saw clouds hovering in the sky.
The fisherman realized that such a paradise on earth was rare,
but he was nevertheless a mere mortal and longed for home.
He left the village then, thinking he could find his way back.
Soon after returning home, he wanted to go back, and left again.
He thought having been there once he could find it with no trouble,
but was surprised to see that everything had changed from before.

He remembered entering the deep forest in the mountain and that
the clear stream, after a few turns, led him into the cloudy trees.
That day too had been in the spring, peach blossoms were everywhere,
even the water was full of them. No way to know now where it went.

桃源行

漁舟逐水愛山春，兩岸桃花夾古津。
坐看紅樹不知遠，行盡青溪不見人。
山口潛行始隈隩，山開曠望旋平陸。
遙看一處攢雲樹，近入千家散花竹。
樵客初傳漢姓名，居人未改秦衣服。
居人共住武陵源，還從物外起田園。
月明松下房櫳靜，日出雲中雞犬喧。
驚聞俗客爭來集，競引還家問都邑。
平明閭巷埽花開，薄暮漁樵乘水入。
初因避地去人間，及至成仙遂不還。
峽裏誰知有人事，世中遙望空雲山。
不疑靈境難聞見，塵心未盡思鄉縣。
出洞無論隔山水，辭家終擬長游衍。
自謂經過舊不迷，安知峰壑今來變。
當時只記入山深，青溪幾曲到雲林。
春來遍是桃花水，不辨仙源何處尋。

Next, we meet our old friend Xishi; she was in *Superstars*. She is the first of the Four Great Beauties of China who was trained to be a spy and sacrificed herself to save her country. In the first three quarters of the poem, he is saying that even though Xishi is beautiful, had she not been noticed, her beauty would have stayed in the Yue village, and she would have lived an ordinary life of obscurity, just like the other washer maids. In the concluding lines, Dong means "east." Since Xi means "west", Xishi and Dongshi are opposites. Without Xishi's charm, that inimitable intangible quality, a frown is just a frown, and can even make one uglier than before.

Now, if we read beauty as a metaphor for talent, and substitute Xishi and the ordinary washer maids with courtiers, we will see that Wang Wei is painting a bigger picture. Read this way, he is saying that if one does not meet the right person who can help one get the attention of the emperor, or those in power, then one's talent will find no use. In other words, many Beethovens have died unnoticed. In the last quarter of the poem, he makes the point that if you don't have the talent to begin with, then forget it, don't even bother trying. His sympathies lie both ways. If he is thinking of the many unrecognized talents, he probably has men like Meng Haoran in mind.

For those who know Li Bai's poem, "Chanting on My Jade Spittoon," it may be a revealing exercise to compare the two poets' use of Xishi's beauty as metaphor in these very different poems by two very different men. Li Bai's poem is in Volume I, p.87-88.

FLOATING ON CLOUDS

A XISHI SONG

The whole world falls for a beautiful face.
Obscurity is not for the likes of a Xishi.
In the morning she was a washer maid at Yue,
by the evening she was the Wu king's favorite.
How different was she from other washer maids,
or did she become special once she was noticed?
It was not the rouge and powder they put on her,
or the pretty silk dresses she was given to wear,
but the king's favor that magnified her charm.
It was his fondness for her that made her faultless.
And what about all those friends she left behind?
Her carriage had no room to take them for a ride.
Tell Dongshi next door it is no use to blindly imitate
that famous frown, no one else has Xishi's charm.

西施詠

豔色天下重，西施寧久微。
朝仍越溪女，暮作吳宮妃。
賤日豈殊眾，貴來方悟稀。
邀人傅香粉，不自著羅衣。
君寵益嬌態，君憐無是非。
當時浣紗伴，莫得同車歸。
持謝鄰家子，效顰安可希。

As often as the Double Ninth or Chong Yang Festival is mentioned in Chinese poetry, and as well-loved as the next Wang Wei poem is, I was quite surprised not to find it in the ten most popular Tang poems cited in the Preamble. The poem is so popular that dogwoods will always bring to mind one's longing for family and especially for brothers in the Chinese culture. This, also, is a poem taught to elementary school children, although I don't remember being told about the dogwood, what it looks like or how it's worn in the hair, maybe I wasn't paying attention in class! As you know, Double Ninth is an autumn festival celebrated by hiking and picnics on high ground, a custom passed on from folklore about escaping danger. Dogwood is supposed to ward off danger, and sprigs of them are passed around for wearing in the hair, in this case among the brothers (Since this is an autumn festival, the sprigs are full of red berries and not flowers). Wang Wei is the eldest of five sons. Shandong is his hometown.

ON DOUBLE NINTH MISSING MY SHANDONG BROTHERS

All alone, feeling like a stranger in a strange place,
doubly missing my family on festival days.
Today my brothers will gather on that familiar hilltop,
pass around dogwood sprigs and find one unclaimed.

九月九日憶山東兄弟

獨在異鄉為異客，
每逢佳節倍思親。
遙知兄弟登高處，
遍插茱萸少一人。

Wang Wei and Pei Di 裴迪

Wang Wei wrote and exchanged many poems with his close friend Pei Di and most of what we know about Pei Di is from this friendship. The most sensational story has to do with how Pei Di saved Wang's life. Apparently, Wang Wei, like Du Fu, was trapped in Chang'an, when the capital fell during the An Lushan Rebellion. Unlike the obscure Du Fu who was left wandering round unnoticed, however, Wang Wei was well-known. An Lushan, therefore, captured him and wanted him to serve his rebel administration. Wang Wei took some mountain herbs and pretended to be ill, but he was not able to evade An Lushan for long and was given an appointment in his court. Wang submitted.

During this time, there was another official of the Tang court, Lei Haiqing, who was a famous pipa player. When Lei was summoned to perform for An, he threw his pipa down, crushed it, turned his face to the south, that is, in the direction of where Emperor Xuanzong had fled, sobbed and refused to play for the rebel. An Lushan ordered him torn limb from limb.

Wang Wei heard about this and felt ashamed. When Pei Di snuck in to visit him in prison at the Boddhi Shrine, he recited the following poem to his friend. Eventually, when Xuanzong's son, Suzong regained control and reestablished the Tang court, Wang was in trouble for having submitted to the rebel. Fortunately for him, his brother, Wang Jin, had been a loyalist and followed the Tang Emperor to the south, and together with Pei Di petitioned on the poet's behalf. Pei Di recited the Boddhi poem to Emperor Suzong, who then pardoned his friend. Some say it was also because of the Wang family's illustrious history with the Tang court that Suzong could not very well have executed him. Here is the poem that saved Wang Wei's life, or so they say.

One more thing, the scholar tree is also called the pagoda tree, which is of the pea family, a deciduous flowering tree that is native to China and Korea. It is also found around Japanese shrines.

MY CHINA IN TANG POETRY

POEM WRITTEN AT BODDHI SHRINE
Recited to Pei Di when he came to visit me and told me how, when the rebel thief threw a banquet at Snow-Jade Pond in Deer Park, our palace musicians all wept while they performed.

Houses are on fire, people wounded, caught in the heat of battle.
How long will it take before our lords will look up at Heaven again?
Leaves are falling from scholar trees, our royal house is empty,
Imperial strings and pipes weep at the banquet at Snow-Jade Pond.

菩提寺禁裴迪來相看說逆賊等凝碧池上作音樂供奉人等
舉聲便一時淚下私成口號誦示裴迪：

萬戶傷心生野煙，
百官何日再朝天。
秋槐葉落空宮裡，
凝碧池頭奏管絃。

After his wife died, Wang Wei remained unmarried for thirty years, very unusual in those days, especially since Wang Wei was a filial son with no one to carry on the family name. His close companion was Pei Di, to whom he wrote and exchanged many poems. The following is one such poem. But first, some background: Master Jie Yu lived during the Spring and Autumn period (475-221 BCE). He was one of those wise men who refused to serve. He cut his hair and feigned madness and lived self-sufficiently as a farmer. As the story goes, he lived the life of an immortal, sustained by drinking dewdrops and riding on clouds. He was the madman who sang in front of Confucius' carriage, ridiculing people who served the political system. He was enshrined as an immortal by the Daoist religion. (Jie Yu can be found in one of Li Bai's ballads written on Mount Lu as well, also included in Volume I, pp. 103-104. Like Pang De, Jie Yu was admired by many of our poets.) Here, Wang Wei was calling his friend, Pei Di, by the name of Jie Yu. From the many poems they exchanged, Pei Di seemed to have come by boat to visit him often at his Web River Retreat. Here Wang Wei was waiting for him at the ferry landing. "Mr. Five Willows" is Tao Qian's nickname because he had written an imaginary autobiography and called himself Mr. Five Willows, saying that there were five dilapidated willows growing by his thatch hut.

FOR MY FRIEND, THE SCHOLAR, PEI DI
In retreat together at Web River

Mountains turning chilly white among the deepening green.
Autumn waters slowing down, flowing gentler by the day.
I lean on my walking stick, waiting at the cottage door,
listening to the crickets' last songs in the windy evening.
At the ferry landing, the sun has almost completely set.
In the village, smoke is rising from many chimneys.
Here comes Master Jie Yu to share a jug with me, and
like Mr. Five Willows, we'll make wild music together.

MY CHINA IN TANG POETRY

輞川閒居贈裴秀才迪

寒山轉蒼翠，
秋水日潺湲。
倚杖柴門外，
臨風聽暮蟬。
渡頭餘落日，
墟里上孤煙。
復值接輿醉，
狂歌五柳前。

What I am calling "Web River Valley" is Wang Chuan, 輞川. (The *wang* 王 in Wang Wei is in the second tone, whereas the *wang* 輞 for both the cartwheel and the web 網 are in the fourth tone. They are three different words). The word *wang* 輞 here means "the outer rim of a cart's wheel", this river runs around the estate like a wheel or circle. If you look at the many reproductions of Wang Wei's paintings of this place you will see what I mean. As it happens, *wang* is homonym of another word that means "net" 網, and if you look at paintings of the various scenes in the estate, a network or web of waterways runs in and out onto this outer ring. I have therefore chosen to call it Web River Valley. This river runs round where Wang Wei bought a village town, which was at Lantian 藍田 (or Blue Fields). Unfortunately for us, after Wang Wei renovated it and made it into a beautiful retreat for himself and his friend Pei Di, he eventually let it go to ruin and nobody came after him to bother about upkeep. At one time, the Web River Retreat was turned into a Buddhist monastery among the many monasteries in the area. In 845, over eight decades after his death, Emperor Wuzong who loathed Buddhism, ordered most of the monasteries in the area destroyed, including Wang Chuan. Wang Wei's paintings of his beautiful retreat were also destroyed.

FLOATING ON CLOUDS

In the Song dynasty, however, a couple of scrolls surfaced, which some claimed to be authentic Wang Wei paintings and collections of his series of poems. Art historians are still unsure. A copy of a 17th century rendition of Wang Wei's original however, can be found at the Freer Gallery of Art in Washington D.C., and since the Song dynasty, many copies of various versions of such paintings have been produced, some of these can be viewed on the internet.

The "Web River Valley Retreat" series of forty poems, half by Wang Wei and half by Pei Di in answer, was written over a period of time at different spots in the estate. At the time, Wang was a part-time official and part-time recluse. After his mother died, he turned the retreat into a monastery or at least shared it with Buddhist monks. In the brief Preface to this series, he tells us that he and Pei Di wrote these poems, harmonizing with each other. I have translated Wang Wei's twenty poems here, but only added Pei Di's response to six of them. A couple of Wang Wei's in this sequence have become very famous. They are all *juejus*.

WEB RIVER VALLEY RETREAT
MENG CITY WALL HOLLOW [Wang Wei writes]

My new home is in the shadow of the city wall,
in the wooded area where a few willows remain.
Hardly anyone comes here anymore these days,
though this town was once a thriving thoroughfare.

MENG CITY WALL HOLLOW [Pei Di's responds]

This thatch hut is within the old city wall.
Sometimes we climb up to take in the view.
The old city is nothing like it used to be,
no one cares, new residents come and go.

MY CHINA IN TANG POETRY

孟城坳

新家孟城口，
古木餘衰柳。
來者復為誰，
空悲昔人有。(王維)

結廬古城下，
時登古城上。
古城非疇昔，
今人自來往。(裴迪)

HILLOCKS AT FLOWER MOUND [Wang Wei writes]

Birds fly away to who knows where,
autumn colors light up the locking hills.
The mountain waves of Flower Mound
overwhelm me with its ups and downs.

HILLOCKS AT FLOWER MOUND [Pei Di responds]

Sun sets and the wind rises among the pines:
heading home through the newly wet grass,
leaving our footprints for misty clouds to fill,
stalks brushing our robes as we walk pass.

華子崗
飛鳥去不窮，
連山復秋色。
上下華子崗，
惆悵情何極。(王維)

FLOATING ON CLOUDS

日落松風起，
還家草露晞。
雲光侵履跡，
山翠拂人衣。(裴迪)

APRICOT STUDIO [Wang Wei writes]

Apricot trees were cut for the rafters,
thick lemongrass braided for the roof.
Under the beams mysterious clouds form
and out into the world they go to make rain.

文杏館

文杏裁為梁，
香茅結為宇。
不知棟裏雲，
去作人間雨。(王維)

    According to Pauline Yu, these "last two lines allude to the second of Guo Pu's (276-324) "Seven Poems on Traveling with Immortals" where there is a couplet that reads "Clouds arise within the rafters;/ Wind emerges from the windows and doors," which describes "the residence of a [D]aoist priest". (See Note to Poem 134 in "The Poetry of Wang Wei," Digital Publication, Indiana University Press.)

BAMBOO RANGE [Wang Wei writes]

Sunlight penetrates the twisty path of the tall green grove.
When wind blows, it sways as if on waves like a pond of lotus.
Further down towards the Mountain Market Road, it runs dark
and mysterious, so dark that even woodcutters lose their way.

斤竹嶺

檀欒映空曲，
青翠漾漣漪。
暗入商山路，
樵人不可知。(王維)

DEER LODGE [Wang Wei writes]

One sees no one on these empty hills,
only human voices punctuate the silence.
Setting rays shine through thickets:
sun-echoes lie on green moss patches.

DEER LODGE [Pei Di responds]

Day and evening on this cold mountain,
I am the only visitor to these parts.
I do not know much about forests,
but I recognize the footprints of stags.

FLOATING ON CLOUDS

鹿柴

空山不見人,
但聞人語響。
返景入深林,
復照青苔上。(王維)

日夕見寒山,
便為獨往客。
不知深林事,
但有麏麚跡。(裴迪)

This little Deer Lodge poem has been translated so many times that there is an article called "Nineteen Ways of Looking at Wang Wei: How a Chinese Poem is Translated," Commentary by Eliot Weinberger, with further comments by Octavio Paz, (Moyer Bell Ltd., 1987). You may find it an interesting exercise to compare them with this twentieth version.

MAGNOLIA LODGE [Wang Wei writes]

Autumn slopes soak in the last rays of sunshine.
Birds fly in pairs, chasing after one another:
Blues and greens shimmering in the light,
like a color storm blowing about, unable to rest.

MY CHINA IN TANG POETRY

MAGNOLIA LODGE [Pei Di's responds]

Feeling lost in the last lights of the sunset,
birds call, confusing the sound of brook waters.
The green-blue river paths twist and turn till
dusk swallows this endless melancholy temper.

木蘭柴

秋山斂餘照,
飛鳥逐前侶。
彩翠時分明,
夕嵐無處所。(王維)

蒼蒼落日時,
鳥聲亂溪水。
緣溪路轉深,
幽興何時已。(裴迪)

ON THE BANKS OF DOGWOOD PLACE [Wang Wei writes]

Their fruits are in reds and greens, so abundant,
it looks like these trees are blooming once again.
When guests arrive to stay in the mountain, they drink
from my wooden cups made from these dogwood trees.

茱萸沜

結實紅且綠,
復如花更開。
山中儻留客,
置此芙蓉杯。(王維)

SCHOLAR TREE PATH [Wang Wei writes]

In the shade of scholar trees a little path is set.
Green moss grows thick under their dark canopy.
I'd tell the groundskeeper not to sweep the moss
except the mountain monk might come for a visit.

SCHOLAR TREE PATH [Pei Di responds]

In front is a shady path under scholar trees
that leads all the way to Interruption Lake,
with autumn coming, it rains often here
at sunset. One cannot sweep up anyway.

宮槐陌

仄徑蔭宮槐，
幽陰多綠苔。
應門但迎掃，
畏有山僧來。(王維)

門前宮槐陌，
是向欹湖道。
秋來山雨多，
落日無人掃。(裴迪)

MY CHINA IN TANG POETRY

KIOSK BY THE LAKE [Wang Wei writes]

I welcome my guests in a little raft.
They arrive, in no hurry, up the lake.
I offer them wine and drink together,
lotus flowers in bloom all around us.

臨湖亭

輕舸迎上客，
悠悠湖上來。
當軒對尊酒，
四面芙蓉開。(王維)

HILLOCKS IN THE SOUTH [Wang Wei writes]

We took a boat to the Hillocks in the South.
Hillocks in the North are too hard to reach.
Across the lake I see people milling about
and wonder who they are, living so close by.

南垞

輕舟南垞去，
北垞淼難即。
隔浦望人家，
遙遙不相識。(王維)

FLOATING ON CLOUDS

INTERRUPTION LAKE [Wang Wei writes]

Flute music travels all the way across the lake.
At day's end, I say goodbye to you, my beloved.
One turn of your head to look backwards to me,
and green hills have rolled into mountain clouds.

欹湖

吹簫凌極浦，
日暮送夫君。
湖上一回首，
山青卷白雲。(王維)

"Wang Wei uses the term 夫君 in the above poem, which is what one calls one's husband, though in archaic Chinese, it can mean "friend".

WILLOW WAVES [Wang Wei writes]

Along both shores willows line up, bow gently
into the clear water, to gaze at their reflections.
Unlike the waterway at the Imperial Palace
where spring winds cut and sharpen goodbyes.

柳浪

分行接綺樹，
倒影入清漪。
不學御溝上，
春風傷別離。(王維)

MY CHINA IN TANG POETRY

LUAN FAMILY SHALLOWS [Wang Wei writes]

Brisk and brittle the autumn wind blows
at the falling water, splattering on rocks.
Jumping waves bounce off each other. Startled,
a pair of white egrets fly and float down again.

欒家瀨

颯颯秋風中，
淺淺石溜瀉。
跳波自相濺，
白鷺驚復下。(王維)

GOLD SPRINKLES SPRING [Wang Wei writes]

Drink some water from Gold Sprinkles Spring each day
and a boy can live till he grows to be a thousand years.
Then the kingfisher phoenix with striped dragons will come
and carry him off in high style to the Jade Emperor's Palace.

金屑泉

日飲金屑泉，
少當千餘歲。
翠鳳翊文螭，
羽節朝玉帝。(王維)

The allusions in this last couplet are to the mythical figures of the Queen Mother of the West (Xi Wang Mu), who rode in a blue phoenix chariot pulled by striped animals. The Jade Emperor is the supreme Daoist deity, a sort of Chinese Zeus. Gold was believed by Daoists to confer immortality, hence their many alchemical experiments. The two gods are sometimes a couple.

WHITE ROCK CASCADE [Wang Wei writes]

White Rock cascades into a shallow pool
where green reeds grow thick under water.
From east and west, families arrive together
to launder their silk under bright moonlight.

白石灘

清淺白石灘，
綠蒲向堪把。
家住水東西，
浣紗明月下。(王維)

HILLOCKS IN THE NORTH [Wang Wei writes]

North of the Northern Hillocks, lake water
turns red from reflections of the many trees,
winding with the curves of River South, by turns
bright and gloomy, ending at the forest's edge.

北坨

北坨湖水北，
雜樹映朱闌。
逶迤南川水，
明滅青林端。(王維)

MY CHINA IN TANG POETRY

BAMBOO GROVE [Wang Wei writes]

Alone in the shades of the bamboo grove
strumming my qin and playing my flute.
Hidden away in the deep forest,
only the moon comes shining in.

BAMBOO GROVE [Pei Di's responds]

Now that I have known Bamboo Grove,
I grow daily closer and closer to the Dao.
Going out and coming in with mountain birds
into the deep woods where no mortals can go.

竹裏館

獨坐幽篁裏，
彈琴復長嘯。
深林人不知，
明月來相照。(王維)

來過竹裏館，
日與道相親。
出入唯山鳥，
幽深無世人。(裴迪)

Lily magnolias are large and hang like bells. Hence, they look "like upside down red sepals of lotus blossoms" in the next poem.

FLOATING ON CLOUDS

LILY MAGNOLIA [Wang Wei writes]

Like upside down red sepals of lotus blossoms hung
on tree branches, they grow all over the mountains.
Does no one live in those silent houses by the river?
Flowers open in rapid succession, then fall, and fall.

辛夷塢

木末芙蓉花，
山中發紅萼。
澗戶寂無人，
紛紛開且落。(王維)

In the next poem, Zhuangzi (Chuangtzu) is the Daoist philosopher who dreamt he was a butterfly, woke up and wondered if he was the butterfly dreaming or dreaming he was a butterfly, to quote the Daoist story most familiar to English readers. He also pretended to be a madman at various times in his life after refusing to come out of hermitage. Apparently, at one time when he agreed to serve, it was in this minor "gardener" capacity. The "few withering trees" will remind those who know Tao Qian and his five willows of that recluse.

LACQUER GARDEN [Wang Wei writes]

Zhuangzi was not too proud to serve, he simply
called himself lacking in worldly experience.
He accepted the appointment to a minor post,
and was happy to tend to a few withering trees.

MY CHINA IN TANG POETRY

漆園

古人非傲吏，
自闕經世務。
偶寄一微官，
婆娑數株樹。(王維)

PEPPER GARDEN [Wang Wei writes]

Setting out the finest crockery fit for a king,
a vaseful of pollias, a sweet gift for my love,
pepper libation served on a jeweled cushion,
everything is ready for the Prince of Clouds.

椒園

桂尊迎帝子，
杜若贈佳人。
椒漿奠瑤席，
欲下雲中君。(王維)

The Retirement Poems

Song Mountain 嵩山 in Henan is one of Wang Wei's several residences at one time or another where he took refuge from the demands of government. He probably went there when he first "retired." His retirement to Zhongnan shan 终南山 is the better known of the two poems you will find in this small selection. These four "retirement" or "hiding" poems are often collected in Wang Wei selections or anthologized in Tang poetry collections. Zhangnanshan is just another name for Nanshan, South Mountain.

FLOATING ON CLOUDS

COMPOSED ON MY WAY HOME TO SONG MOUNTAIN

The clear brook flows alongside a patch of grassy woodland.
My carriage rides alongside, as leisurely as its water flows.
The sound of this water is like a song sung with warm feelings,
as evening birds find their nests while I am returning home.
Few people live in this ancient city, once a busy thoroughfare.
A setting sun is gradually taking over the autumn mountains.
I am retiring to the distant foothills of majestic Song Mountain:
there is where I shall close my door to worldly fret and care.

歸嵩山作

清川帶長薄，
車馬去閒閒。
流水如有意，
暮禽相與還。
荒城臨古渡，
落日滿秋山。
迢遞嵩高下，
歸來且閉關。

MY CHINA IN TANG POETRY

EVENING FALLS AT THE MOUNTAIN LODGING

An empty mountain newly washed in rain
feels like fall as the evening descends on us.
A bright moon peers through stands of pines,
clear spring water ripples over liquid rocks.
From the bamboo grove come girls' voices:
they must be going home after washing clothes.
Lotus fronds rock gently on the sudden waves:
must be fishing boats pushing out for the night.
Spring flowers are gone for now, I have no regrets.
This is a good place for a gentleman to stay a while.

山居秋暝

空山新雨後，
天氣晚來秋，
明月松間照，
清泉石上流。
竹喧歸浣女，
蓮動下魚舟，
隨意春芳歇，
王孫自可留。

In the above translation I have done something I rarely do. I have translated lines five and six in the Chinese with four lines. The economy of the Chinese lines are simply too difficult to overcome. The Chinese lines read: "bamboo make-noise = returning washing girls" and "lotus moving = fishing boats go out." Thus, the English here has ten lines versus the original eight lines of the Chinese original.

FLOATING ON CLOUDS

RETIREMENT TO SOUTH MOUNTAIN

In my middle years I found an interest in the Dao,
so I have retired here to the slopes of South Mountain.
When the mood arises, I would take off all by myself
to a place I know where nothingness is my sole pleasure.
I walk all the way to the top of the river, to a spot where
I sit, watching clouds rise up from nowhere to the sky.
Occasionally an old woodcutter walks out of the woods,
and we would start chatting and laughing the day away.

終南別業

中歲頗好道，
晚家南山陲。
興來每獨往，
勝事空自知。
行到水窮處，
坐看雲起時。
偶然值林叟，
談笑無還期。

MY CHINA IN TANG POETRY

THANKING MASTER ZHANG WITH A POEM [1]

I tend to love quiet now in my evening years,
not caring much about much in the world.
Making no long-term plans, I just keep to myself.
Emptied of knowledge, I have returned to the woods.
A breeze blows through the pines, loosening my robe.
The mountain moon is my lamplight for playing the qin.
You ask for the secret of transcending all worldly matter:
just listen to the fisherman's song coming down the river.

酬張少府

晚年唯好靜,
萬事不關心。
自顧無長策,
空知返舊林。
松風吹解帶,
山月照彈琴。
君問窮通理,
漁歌入浦深。

Let us say goodbye to Wang Wei with one of his most popular poems. By "popular" I do not mean that it is the most representative or even the most famous of Wang Wei's poems. I mean that, of all his poems, it is the most used by the populace. I believe it would be difficult, even today, to find a teenage girl growing up in Chinese society who is unfamiliar with this song. I can still hear my teenage sister, who had a very good singing voice, singing this song at one of our many gatherings with

---

1   This poem appeared in the September 2023 Issue of *Poetry Magazine*.

friends when we were growing up.

   Originally set to the music of the guqin, it is sung at farewell gatherings, usually repeated three times in a variety of ways. Thus, it is sometimes called Yang Guan San Die (Sun's Gate [Pass] Three Times Repeated.) The earliest musical score is found in 1491, and the most popular version used is the one composed in the Qing dynasty in 1864. We have no evidence that Wang Wei scored it himself, even though he was an accomplished musician. It is also often quoted by others in their poems when saying goodbye:

A FAREWELL SONG AT THE CITY OF WEI

Morning rain has washed clean the dust-filled air.
New willows by the guest house are green again.
Come, have another drink with me before you go.
Beyond Sun's Gate nobody will know your name.

渭城曲

渭城朝雨浥輕塵，
客舍青青柳色新。
勸君更盡一杯酒，
西出陽關無故人。

3

Li Ye 李冶 (737? – 784)
This Music Knows No End

There is no record of when exactly Li Ye (courtesy name, Li Jilan) was born. We do know, however, when she died. The year was 784. We know this because she was executed and there was a record of it. We also know that she was a famous nun. During most of the Tang dynasty, Daoist nuns were well-respected, because Li Yuan, founder of the dynasty, claimed to be descended from Laozi, the father of Daoism. To become a Daoist nun meant that one would not be following the Confucian path to womanhood, which prescribed marriage and children, and accepting certain social norms, like behaving with restraint with men other than one's husband and following Confucian decorum. Moreover, being a Daoist nun did not entail, it would seem, renouncing all material comfort and expectations of enjoyment, nor is celibacy demanded, as it is of the Buddhist clergy. Indeed, other than proving oneself religiously inclined by passing some tests in the scriptures, the calling paradoxically freed one to pursue such interests as literary and philosophical studies, music, calligraphy, and other art forms traditionally denied women. One also became financially independent of father and husband because the land-equalization system, which the Tang dynasty adopted, conferred acreage to these women via the Daoist temples to which they belonged. Thus, the power and mystique of the Daoist nun peaked in the Tang dynasty.

According to Tang official statistics, there were 1,687 Daoist temples in the 8th Century: 1,137 for men and 550 for women. This, however, does not mean that Buddhism did not also enjoy tremendous growth in power and influence. Suffice it here to say that both these teachings and Confucianism were equally important to Chinese cultural life, and though Buddhism and Daoism (Taoism) seem to be in competition for hearts and minds, there is also quite a bit of crossover in their philosophies. Thus, you see the concept of "dao" being thrown about without being clearly designated as one or the other of them and the concept is also important in Confucianism and later, even Christianity. I imagine everyone wants to know "the Way". In other words, women made up an important part of the Daoist clergy. The rise of aristocratic Daoist nuns during this time was also unprecedented in Chinese history. Even the Imperial households counted Daoist clergy among them. At least twelve princesses became ordained Daoist nuns, and their imperial residences were converted into nunneries. This way, they were relieved from their social obligations but maintained their political influence and avoided palace intrigues. They became economically independent and were able to pursue scholarly studies and various arts as they wished. They were also able to achieve a degree of personal freedom to travel and enjoy the company of men that other women could have only imagined during this time. There were also stories told about their licentious way of life, some true and some fantastical. Some of these stories are like those found in our sleazier tabloids. Most of the poets you are meeting in this volume have made the acquaintance of Daoist nuns, either for esoteric conversations or myriad other kinds of entertainment. (Most of the above information is from Despeux, Catherine.

"Women in Daoism," in Kohn, Livia, ed., *Daoism Handbook*. (Brill Academic Publication (2005)).

Despite the attractiveness of the vocation, however, most parents would still normally have wanted their daughters to be married and have families. Indeed, Confucian norms dominated social life until Mao took over centuries later, and in some traditional families it still does. It is, therefore, unusual that Li Ye's father chose this path for his daughter when she was only eleven years old. Posterity has been given two explanations. One is that it was not her father's choice, but that her father died, and her mother fell into poverty and had no way to support her. The other explanation is more interesting and therefore generally the story told. Apparently, she was an extremely bright child, a prodigy even, and at age six surprised her father by coming up with a poem that made a pun on "trellis" 架 and "a woman's marriage" 嫁 which are homophones, both pronounced *jia*. The poem is about climbing roses, sometimes used to describe women who step out of bounds by having extramarital relationships, or at least have thoughts of them. The father worried. On top of that, Li Ye was also apparently an unruly child, willful and too clever for her own good. The father worried some more, and eventually decided that the nunnery, and therefore a life without marriage, would be the safest place for her as she approached puberty.

A happier view of this decision would be that he appreciated her talents and realized that the nunnery was a better place for her artistic and intellectual development than at home or in a marriage. If this was indeed the case, he was not wrong. Li Ye became an accomplished scholar, poet, and qin player. Indeed, it was her talent which enabled her to entertain with eloquence that made scholars young and old seek her out for companionship. She became a star, if you will, and eventually even Emperor Daizong

(Xuanzong's grandson) heard and sent for her. Unfortunately, according to the story, by the time he brought her to the palace she was already over the hill. He was sorely disappointed as she did not live up to her reputation of being a nubile young thing, in addition to being an exceptional poet and musician. After only a month at the palace, she was sent away.

During her lifetime, Li Ye met many literary men. She was able to respond to their poems in kind, something the literati appreciated, especially after a few drinks. You had a glimpse of this from the "Web River Retreat" sequence between Wang Wei and Pei Di. They answered one another back and forth with poems and were especially delighted when a beautiful woman unexpectedly answered them back with her own compositions or conducted witty conversations without shyness or ignorance. Indeed, as the story goes, Li Ye lived up to the challenge every time. Sometimes these gatherings were raunchy, but Li Ye was able to handle herself well, and go toe to toe with the men, whether it was quoting from the classics or making unsavory jokes, with wit and subtlety. Depending on who you believe, Li Ye either had many lovers -- even propositioning a monk once, who regrettably chose Buddha over her -- or else she kept these men in platonic relationships with her. The monumental and rather graphic event in this not entirely unhappy life (though quite a lonely one at times as her poems attest) came at the very end, when a rebel general temporarily deposed the Tang emperor. During that short time when the general was in power, he heard about Li Ye and her talents, and since he was also a fan of good poetry, made her write in praise of him at the expense of the Tang emperor. When Emperor Dezong, Daizong's son, recovered the throne for the Tang dynasty, he could not forgive her for obeying the scoundrel and ordered that she be "bludgeoned to death by indiscriminate thrashes". This was an actual legal punishment.

MY CHINA IN TANG POETRY

She was not as fortunate as Wang Wei under a different emperor's reign, even though his offense was not that different than hers.

Most of her poems have now been lost, although once upon a time she collected them in a volume under her own name. All we have now are eighteen poems that were gathered by a Song dynasty scholar. Most of these poems were either about missing somebody who had been a friend or lover, or poems written on the occasion of someone, friend or lover, leaving her. There must also have been many poems written for special occasions. She was, after all, "just a woman".

Li Ye gave the title of 相思怨, "Longing Complaint/Grievance", to the following poem, perhaps to distinguish it from the kind of longing poems we see so often in Tang poetry called "長相思," which, since there are no singular or plural designations in classical Chinese, can be translated as "Thinking of You Thinking of Me". In this case, however, the longing is not necessarily reciprocal, and may not yield any results. Thus, the "complaint/grief" 怨. Also, the kind of "complaint" the word "怨" evokes places it squarely in the genre of women's poetry, as in 閨怨, spoken by one confined to the boudoir or bed chamber. Moreover, the word she uses for "shore" in the fourth line is 畔 which, though not an exact pun on 伴 or companion, in modern Mandarin, has the same pronunciation in Cantonese and some other regional dialects, and shares the radical 半, which means half, or other half. All this to say, she has no other half, or at least cannot be sure that the man she is longing for is also longing for her.

FLOATING ON CLOUDS

LONGING FOR MY LOVE: A COMPLAINT

People say the ocean is deep,
not half as deep as my longing.
Ocean waters end with the horizon,
my endless longing has no other shore.
I would take my qin to the high tower,
and play to that faraway, vacant moon,
but the bright moon is deaf to my music.
I fear my strings will break from longing.

相思怨

人道海水深，
不抵相思半。
海水尚有涯，
相思渺無畔。
攜琴上高樓，
樓虛月華滿。
彈著相思曲，
弦腸一時斷。

Hints of "normal" womanly interests are visible in these poems even though she was not an ordinary woman anymore, but a nun. For example, in this poem, the silk remnants are from sewing and the knot-tying is a "female" activity. Carp, like wild geese, are metaphors for letters, also letter bringers or messengers. In other words, she had written him a letter and sent it in the silk carp's belly. Sending letters in a pair of carps is a reference to an ancient story. Knot-tying is like origami only done with fabric and shaped into all kinds of animals and other ornamental things. Also, "tying" as it happens, has the same implication as in the English expression, "tying the knot"!

A PAIR OF SILK CARPS FOR A FRIEND

White silk remnants like leftover snow,
good for tying knots into a pair of carps.
If you wish to know what is in my heart,
open a carp and look for it in its belly.

結素魚貽友人

尺素如殘雪，
結為雙鯉魚。
欲知心裡事，
看取腹中書。

Li Ye is not above name-dropping, and in the next poem, she tells us Lu Hongjiang, aka Lu Yu 陸羽, a prominent poet-official, is a friend. Lu Yu is nicknamed the "Tea Saint" because he was a connoisseur. In the poem, she also alludes to Tao Qian, the much admired ancient recluse and drinker, and Xie Lingyun, Tao's counterpart, well-known for his mountain and river poems and a seasoned traveler.

FLOATING ON CLOUDS

DRIFTING ON THE LAKE, STILL FEELING SICK, AND HAPPENED UPON LU HONGJIAN

When you left, frost was shrouding the moon.
Now that you're here, a thick fog has rolled in.
So happy we meet again, though I have fallen ill.
So much I want to say: tears get in the way of words.
Celebrating the recluse who loved a drink or two,
reciting verses from that old traveler just for fun,
we should get drunk together at this chance reunion.
There can't possibly be anything else you'd rather do.

湖上臥病喜陸鴻漸至

昔去繁霜月，
今來苦霧時。
相逢仍臥病，
欲語淚先垂。
強勸陶家酒，
還吟謝客詩。
偶然成一醉，
此外更何之。

Not all relationships can be casual and flirty like that one though, and the following few attest to her loneliness.

MY CHINA IN TANG POETRY

UNDER THE BRIGHT MOON

The one who is leaving does not speak. The moon is also silent.
The moon hoards its brightness. The man carries his love hidden.
After we part, the longing will start, and we will be like the moon,
floating on clouds, floating on the water, farther and farther apart.

明月夜留別

離人無語月無聲，
明月有光人有情。
別後相思人似月，
雲間水上到層城。

The Chinese title to the next poem, is 偶居 *ou ju*, meaning living together. Since cohabitation is not likely for a nun, I am guessing this is someone who stayed a short while at the nunnery with her. She was known to fall in love at various times with various people. Her nunnery was called the Southern Hill Abbey. It was not unusual for travelers, mostly scholars or officials, to stay at monasteries and nunneries for short periods of time, either for respite, retreat, or when traveling. Li Bai stayed at a princess nun's residence at one point, for example., and even Wang Wei was known to have befriended a few nuns.

FLOATING ON CLOUDS

A SHORT STAY

My heart is with that far cloud wherever it has gone.
Nothing came between us when we were together.
Then, a stormy wind rose up and blew us asunder,
forcing one to the southern hills and one to the north.

偶居

心遠浮雲知不還，
心雲併在有無間。
狂風何事相搖蕩，
吹向南山復北山。

Being a spiritual adviser was one of her official roles as a Daoist nun. In the last couplet of this next poem, we find a hint of the competition with Buddhism that is always present between the two religions. This philosophical or religious poem was either a gift she gave to one of her clients or it was requested by him as he departed for an official post.

DAOIST SENTIMENTS SENT TO MINISTER CUI

Do not be stuck on making a name, it's but a fleeting thing.
Official duties should be done without getting too attached.
A hundred years is but a day, less than a moment in a day,
what you achieve in the past or future is nothing in the end.
Your hair will turn white no matter what you do, why worry.
Looking young just means you have not yet studied enough.
There's no need to go all the way to India to find sacred texts,
wisdom can be found right here at home with the old masters.

MY CHINA IN TANG POETRY

道意寄崔侍郎

莫漫戀浮名，
應須薄宦情。
百年齊旦暮，
前事盡虛盈。
愁鬢行看白，
童顏學未成。
無過天竺國，
依止古先生。

I have resorted to adding a phrase, "less than a moment in a day," to lengthen that line in order to make my little box pattern for these even line length poems. This is a confession to a translator's occasional "sin", not casually embarked upon, nor normally forgiven.

SENT TO ZHU FANG

Gazing on the lake as I clamber up the mountain.
A mountain so high, a lake so wide, as immense
as my longing for you. Endless nights, and days
turning into endless gazing into months and years.
The mountain is rich with brilliant forest greenery.
Wildflowers surround me overwhelming my senses.
After you left, I was left with infinite longing.
When next we meet, I'll have so much to say.

FLOATING ON CLOUDS

寄朱放

望水試登山，
山高湖又闊。
相思無曉夕，
相望經年月。
郁郁山木榮，
綿綿野花發。
別後無限情，
相逢一時說。

  Some have suggested that this Zhu Fang (sometimes given as 朱昉) is the closest she ever came to calling someone husband. Still, he didn't come back in the end.

  Daoist nuns are allowed to leave their vocation and get married. Remember those emperors who retrieved the nuns they wanted for themselves from the nunneries? I am talking about the two most famous ones, China's one and only Empress, Wu Zetian, and her grandson's Imperial Consort, Yang Guifei, whose stories were told in *Superstars*. Li Ye, as evidenced in these poems, has daydreamed about marriage. The next poem is about marital relationships. I am including two versions of my translations here. The first title is closer to the Chinese, but I like the possibility of the second version as well. You decide which you prefer. One wonders how she came to know so much about marriage, being a nun.

MY CHINA IN TANG POETRY

First Version:

EIGHT MOSTS

Most near, most far: from east to west.
Most deep, most shallow: clear brook water.
Most high, most bright: the sun and the moon.
Most dear, most unknowable: husband and wife.

Second Version:

EIGHT SOMETIMES

As near, as far, as East to West,
as deep, as shallow, as clear brook water,
as high, as bright, as the sun and moon,
as close, as remote, as husband and wife.

八至

至近至遠東西,
至深至淺清溪。
至高至明日月,
至親至疏夫妻。

In this next poem, Li Ye seems to be describing her appreciation of a famous master's performance on the qin. Being an excellent qin player herself, it is reasonable to assume that her appreciation is greater than the normal listener's. As we read on, we find that this was a private performance that took place in her room. Again, since the composition describes "the music of the Three Gorges," it would be reasonable for her to claim familiarity with the sound of its music, to the extent of comparing herself to the goddess who lived in the mountains. That would be one way of understanding this poem.

On the other hand, since Song Yu's ancient story about the Goddess of Wushan, which I have translated as Goddess of Witch Mountain here and elsewhere, is well-known, one should immediately be alerted to what her claim in the opening of the poem implies. Moreover, since Daoist nuns had the reputation of being aficionados in sexual matters, and the euphemism, "cloud and rain," was already almost a cliché for intercourse by then, we can safely assume that the double entendre one can hear in the poem is not accidental. Plus, this master could, by a small stretch of the imagination, have been a lover to Li Ye, as well as a master qin player.

ON HEARING XIAO SHUZI PLAY
THE MUSIC OF THE THREE GORGES ON THE QIN

> The clouds of Witch Mountain were once my home;
> the sound of lively water filled my senses every day.
> Now the music from your qin has brought back to me
> that song the Three Gorges used to sing in my dreams.
> So far in the distance those waters are flowing, yet
> tonight, it was as if they flowed through my room.
> Your fingers have brought to life those giant boulders
> and the strings are like water spray and running waves.
> One moment comes the roar of thunder rushing by,
> then water whimpering in a tight crevice of a cliff.
> Loud like rage, soft like sobbing, working its way down,
> gradually gliding, soaking slowly into smooth sand.
> In days of old when Master Yuan played this tune,
> the virtuous men at court could never have enough,

asking him to play it over and over again, just like the waters of the Gorges, this music knows no end.

從蕭叔子聽彈琴，賦得三峽流泉歌

妾家本住巫山雲，巫山流泉常自聞。
玉琴彈出轉寥夐，直是當時夢裏聽。
三峽迢迢幾千裏，一時流入幽閨裏。
巨石崩崖指下生，飛泉走浪弦中起。
初疑憤怒含雷風，又似嗚咽流不通。
回湍曲瀨勢將盡，時復滴瀝平沙中。
憶昔阮公爲此曲，能令仲容聽不足。
一彈既罷復一彈，願作流泉鎮相續。

4

Xue Tao 薛濤 (768 – 831)
Waiting, Dreaming, Hoping

Xue Tao's father was a scholar official. She was born in 768 and was his only child. He loved her, as the saying goes, "like the bright pearl in his palm". For the first fourteen years of her life, the family lived in Chang'an, the capital. Like Li Ye, Xue Tao was also a prodigy. Her story is as follows. Her father came up with a couplet one day that went

> In our garden grows an old wutong,
> reaching all the way into the clouds.

At which point, somebody answered with a complementary couplet:

> Its branches welcome birds from north and south.
> Its leaves wave to the wind coming and going by.

Astonished by the childish voice that pronounced it, he looked round and saw his eight-year-old daughter. This kind of "test" – giving the first couplet and asking for an answering couplet to match it – is often used to see if a fellow scholar is up to snuff, and here, a little girl was able to respond in kind to her father and

MY CHINA IN TANG POETRY

astonished him. He was one of those open-minded and outspoken kinds of officials. The first characteristic made him open to educating his daughter, and the second, as is wont to happen, got him demoted and sent away to Sichuan, where the hot food comes from. Thereafter, they lived in Chengdu, the hub of Shu, as it was still called. If you remember Shu from Li Bai's "The Road to Shu is Hard", you will recall that this was quite a center of entertainment, even though it was not Chang'an. Unfortunately, the year Xue Tao turned fourteen, her father contracted a serious illness and died. For two years, mother and daughter lived close to poverty. When she turned sixteen, they decided, with her beauty and talents, especially when it came to poetry, to enter her into the Guild of Courtesans, that is, a school set up to train young women to entertain "educated gentlemen". Courtesans in the Tang dynasty were not prostitutes, even though they were in the "entertainment business". There was a wide range of abilities among the Tang courtesans; they were mostly well-educated and well-trained to entertain, but not all were skilled in the arts. You might compare these courtesans to geishas or oirans, high-class courtesans in Japan in the Edo period, which came much later than these Chinese courtesans. In China at that time, they were "official" entertainers who were supported by the Imperial court and could be summoned to entertain at the capital.

It was at the guild that she was discovered by Wei Gao, a former general who became the military governor of the Xichuan Circuit in Chengdu, who made her the hostess of his headquarters where she was to meet the likes of Bai Juyi and Yuan Zhen, among other scholar-officials, either when they were still candidates on their way to take that pesky Imperial Exam or after they were already scholar-officials stationed thereabouts.

Wei Gao so admired her writing talents that he even tried to persuade the emperor to appoint her *jiaoshu* (usually translated as editor of court documents). This did not come to pass because the post had never been held by a woman, but since she was presented to the emperor and it was known that Wei Gao recommended her for the position, those who knew her started addressing her as "female editor" (a compliment). Her fame traveled far and wide, and she became too full of herself. Some years into her appointment as Wei Gao's hostess, she succumbed to the temptation of taking bribes for her services. This enraged Wei Gao when he found out and he sent her away to Songzhou in the boonies. On her way there, she wrote the set of "Ten Parted Poems", which, as the story goes, reminded the old man how much he loved her and he sent for her again.

In 809, when she was forty-one, she met Yuan Zhen 元稹, who was eleven years her junior. She was now past her prime, but poetry knows no age barrier, and the two fell in love, or so we're told. Yuan Zhen, who, you will soon learn, was quite the Don Juan, had to go back to the capital, and after he left, they exchanged poems for a while, but the aspiring poet scholar-official became "realistic" and never came back for her. She left the entertainment profession then and became a Daoist nun, retiring to what has now become a tourist spot.

Of the four women poets we meet here, she is probably the most popularly remembered. There are several reasons for this. First, at the time of her death, there were still as many as four hundred fifty poems in a collection of her poetry called *Brocade River*, after the river by that name in Chengdu, and these survived until the 14th Century. Today, we still have about ninety to a hundred of them. Second, since she exchanged poems with so many famous Tang poets, and she lived relatively long, into her sixties, she was better known than her contemporary women poets. Third, she was also an inventor who developed a paper product still called Xue Tao Note today. It is a pinkish rice paper tinted with color

MY CHINA IN TANG POETRY

from the hibiscus and finer than other paper made in Chengdu at the time. There is a well in or near her residence called the Xue Tao Well, which is supposed to have been the source of the water she used to make this paper. She used to write her poems on this paper and sent them to various poets. And there is a fourth reason. In late Qing dynasty, in 1889, a four-story tower called Wang Jiang Lou (River Gazing Tower) was built at the Wang Jiang Park, where a statue of Xue Tao can be found among many species of bamboos (more than 150 kinds, according to the tour book), in memory of her, as she loved bamboo. In other words, beyond her poetry, her memory is kept very much alive by tourism. And last but not least, her residence is not far from Du Fu's thatch hut. In addition, this is beautiful country where many landmarks in poetry throughout the ages are found, many familiar to you in this series: Moth Brow Mountain (Emei Shan), Leshan with its giant buddha, the archeological site of Sanxingdui, numerous temples, and of course, pandas.

Xue Tao died in 831. She was sixty-two years old, give or take a year or two. On her tombstone was engraved the title "Nu Jiaoshu" ("Female Editor").

We begin with one of her better known five-character *juejus*. It is probably an early poem and could have been written with any number of men in mind. Since she was talking about building a nest and looking forward to children, she would have been quite young. Remember, in those days, fourteen or fifteen was already marriageable age. The last line is both subtle and obvious as to what the couple is busy about, other than preparing a nest. The word-for-word translation of the line is: one heart/lotus leaves/ among, meaning, "[we] are as one (or share one heart) among the lotus leaves."

FLOATING ON CLOUDS

LOVE BIRDS IN THE LOTUS POND

Nesting on the pond's green foliage,
from dawn to dusk they come and go,
looking forward to when chicks arrive:
a busy couple among the lotus leaves.

池上雙鳥

雙棲綠池上，
朝暮共飛還。
更憶將雛日，
同心蓮葉間。

HONEYSUCKLE

Intertwining green vines clinging on the steps,
spreading sweet smell in gold and silver pairs,
enjoying the long days of spring into summer,
forgetting that autumn wind will soon be here.

鴛鴦草

綠英滿香砌，
兩兩鴛鴦小。
但娛春日長，
不管秋風早。

In Chinese, honeysuckle is called "mandarin duck grass" or "gold and silver blossoms" because of its coloring. Mandarin ducks, or yuanyangs, are symbolic of lovers, especially at play, and because they mate for life or so they thought.

MY CHINA IN TANG POETRY

If these were poems written for herself or addressed to one other person – we might call them private poems – there are others, written to entertain an audience. We can call those public poems or party poems. Party poems are those that the hostess, probably after everyone has had a few, invites the scholars to make verses with her. There are many poetry games of this sort, although in recent years fewer and fewer people are able to play them. The first of the following verse does not give a subject or topic, so the participants would probably be asked to match it prosodically. Other games might begin with the host or hostess reciting a couple of lines from a well-known poem or from a couplet he or she makes up on the spot. Then, others are challenged to complete another couplet to resonate with it. Sometimes, a title or subject is proposed, and participants are invited to write poems to compete one with another. Sometimes there are prosodic rules to follow, and these can be strict or forgiving. We are not aware if any was given for the following game. It is easy to forget, but they are partying at a nunnery, "a place of *chan [or zen]*", as she called it. Moreover, they have been drinking, and the double entendre here about her little stream and their rivers of poetry also suggest the by-product of drinking, that is, urination. Pretty raunchy, eh?

INVITING EVERY GENTLEMAN PRESENT TO PARTICIPATE

Lift your voices and join me in the following song.
Even though my little stream cannot compete with
your ample rivers, I will try my best to fulfill my duty
and we'll fill this place of chan with a flood of poetry.

FLOATING ON CLOUDS

宣上人見示與諸公唱和

許廁高齋唱，
涓泉定不如。
可憐譙記室，
流水滿禪居。

"Description or appreciation of things" in poetry, is sort of like "still life" in painting. It is a genre in Chinese poetry, as in "In Praise of Such and Such," or *yong wu*, 咏 物. As stated above, these topics could be used for games as well. The following poems could be used at parties to start off a competition or they were poetic exercises Xue Tao set for herself. We can imagine that courtesans like Xue Tao have a collection of these to use whenever the occasion calls for them. We can also imagine the courtesan pretending to come up with the topic and the poem extemporaneously, recite one from memory and thus appear supersmart.

BREEZE

Orchids play a game of catch in the gentle breeze.
Music of strumming strings invites answering calls.
From high branches come the twitter of bird songs.
A night wind whistles through the pine-strewn path.

風

獵蕙微風遠，
飄弦哦一聲。
林梢鳴淅瀝，
松徑夜悽清。

MY CHINA IN TANG POETRY

As in that carp poem by Li Ye, the weaving activity in the next poem identifies the speaker of the poem (and the moon) as female; knot-tying and weaving are both the work, or hobby of women. Circle fans, as the name implies, are fans made in the shape of a circle.

MOON

A sliver of new moon like a hook has just begun
to weave itself into the fullness of a circle fan.
When this skinny light becomes round and bright,
singly or together, we will be returning its gaze.

月

魄依鈎樣小，
扇逐漢機團。
細影將圓質，
人間幾處看。

CICADAS

Dewdrops and cicada sounds, clear and crisp,
join in the chorus of wind-blown leaves.
Each note seems to harmonize with another,
though each comes from a different tree.

FLOATING ON CLOUDS

蟬

露滌清音遠，
風吹故葉齊。
聲聲似相接，
各在一枝棲。

You may also have noticed by now that Chinese poets love nature, the seasons, and natural scenery in general. Many plants, flowers especially, are symbolic, and many real flowers and plants are cultivated, and people have intimate or at least nostalgic associations of them. Many scholar-poets have gardens in their residences, the rich ones certainly have them, but even the poor have special feelings for plants in their courtyards, and if not courtyards, at least potted plants in whatever little space they have.

Scholars, especially, love rocks and stones. There are people who collect them, as one would collect artwork. There is a genre called "Strange Rocks" (*qi shi* 奇石) and hobbyists collect rocks that resemble or remind them of other things. Rock gardens are everywhere, and again, these are made to resemble naturally occurring phenomena. Perhaps this whole rock or stone culture is encouraged and inspired by the many fantastic mountains in China. No wonder people like the Tang poets we have been meeting go hiking all the time, and here, in these chapters on the "Four Talented Females" of the Tang dynasty, we see that even the women love to go to these high places. At least they didn't have to hobble around on three-inch lotuses like those in the Song dynasty when foot-binding came into vogue.

Bamboo, pine, and plum trees or flowers, are considered our "Three Friends of Winter," so-called because they can survive in winter and provide those who admire them with a quiet reminder of living things which, for the most part at this time of year, are either dead, dormant, or in hibernation. The following poem is in praise of one of the three friends. Virtuous scholars are compared to bamboo in their strength, endurance, growth, and moral integrity, among other good things, and bamboo brings to mind the "Seven Sages of the Bamboo Grove" whom you can find in the Meng Haoran chapter. In the following poem, they are called "the drinkers of Jin." The dispassionate heart or hollow heart in the Chinese is both a physical description of the bamboo stalk and the metaphoric meaning of its purity; because the bamboo trunk has nothing in it, i.e., no desire, and therefore incorruptible. The desire-free or empty heart is also a Daoist concept. "Bamboo after rain" 雨後春筍 is an idiom meaning rapid growth. The story about the Shun sisters is often found in Chinese poems. The sisters' story was used by Li Bai in his poem, "Torn Away", for example, which is found in Volume I. Briefly, they were the loyal sisters who were married to the Sage King, Shun, and who, when he died, cried so hard that their tears turned to drops of blood splattered onto the bamboo grove nearby. The leaves on these bamboo thereafter have red spots on them.

ADMIRING BAMBOO AFTER RAIN, FOR MY GUESTS' AMUSEMENT

A bamboo grove after spring rain is a sight to behold
but cannot compare to its poise and beauty in the snow.
There are other trees that flourish in every season
but who else has the bamboo's dispassionate heart?
Chosen by the drinkers of Jin as their gathering spot.
Splattered with tears of the sisters who served Shun.
They stand tall and unbending in their radiant green,
calling to mind the virtues of endurance and integrity.

FLOATING ON CLOUDS

酬人雨後玩竹

南天春雨時，
那鑑雪霜姿。
眾類亦云茂，
虛心寧自持。
多留晉賢醉，
早伴舜妃悲。
晚歲君能賞，
蒼蒼勁節奇。

The next poem has to be understood with the story she referred to in its last line. It is the story of 羅敷 Luo Fu. Hers is an ancient tale, so ancient, in fact, her name has come to mean a beautiful and true young woman, possibly married but most likely not. The story is from one of the poems in the *Book of Songs*, or *Shijing*, the oldest book of Chinese poetry, made up of mostly folksongs. According to the poem, Mo Shang Sang 陌上桑, "Mulberry on the Road," Luo Fu was a young woman who picked mulberry for a living, or she just happened to be picking mulberries by the road when a soldier passed by on the Eastern Road. She was so beautiful that he wanted her to come with him and be his concubine. She replied immediately, putting him in his place, saying something like, "How stupid you are! You who have a wife, and I, a husband." She proceeded to paint a picture of some high up, handsome, leader of men, (one who would ride at the head of the pack) and sent the poor guy on his way. Thereafter, people call exceptionally beautiful young women who are loyal to their husbands, real or ideal, true or imagined, Luo Fu.

It is somewhat arrogant of Xue Tao, an unmarried entertainer, albeit a very successful one, to thus describe herself. She did, however, put Prefect Zheng at the head of his line of soldiers on the Eastern Road. Perhaps she was saying that he was "husband material"? It is more than likely that this poem was written when Xue Tao was still flying high, before Wei Gao sent her away.

FAREWELL TO PREFECT ZHENG OF MEIZHOU
Falling rain has darkened Mei Mountain's paths and waterways.
From this tower, I watch you go, hiding tears behind my sleeve.
Banners flying on Eastern Road, a thousand riders in double files,
but I, like Luo Fu, only have eyes for the one at the head of the line.

送鄭眉州

雨暗眉山江水流，
離人掩袂立高樓。
雙旌千騎駢東陌，
獨有羅敷望上頭。

Following are five of the "Ten Parted Poems" she wrote when Wei Gao sent her away to Songzhou. Although some commentators have surmised that they were written to Yuan Zhen, I prefer the former conjecture, especially as I find some of them rather demeaning. The whiny, begging tone sounds more like an inferior writing a master to petition her return to luxury, rather than a lover's lament.

FLOATING ON CLOUDS

TEN PARTED POEMS
1 DOG PARTED FROM MASTER

My master kept me warm in his house for four, five years, my fur was scented, and my paws cleaned, he loved me so. For no reason at all, I bit my master's close friend one day, and now I have lost my comfortable, carpeted red silk bed.

十離詩
其一：犬離主

馴擾朱門四五年，
毛香足淨主人憐；
無端咬着親情客，
不得紅絲毯上眠。

In the next poem, Yue and Xuan are where the best bamboo and animal hair for paint and calligraphy brushes come from. "Red petals" here are words. Wang Xizhi 王羲之 is the famous calligrapher who lived in the Jin dynasty from 303-361 C.E.

2 BRUSH PARTED FROM HAND

Bamboo from Yue and hair from Xuan were lovingly made into this superior brush, as it scattered red petals with fine ink. From much use its supple tip is worn thin and no longer worthy of the calligrapher Wang Xizhi's famous strokes.

MY CHINA IN TANG POETRY

其二：筆離手

越管宣毫始稱情，
紅箋紙上撒花瓊。
都緣用久鋒頭盡，
不得羲之手裏擎。

3 HORSE PARTED FROM BARN

Ears of snow and a coat of red with jade hooves on my feet,
I chased the wind from the bright sun's east to its farthest west.
Since my master fell off my back as I reared up from a fright,
I am not allowed near him, my voice not heard at his door.

其三：馬離廄

雪耳紅毛淺碧蹄，
追風曾到日東西。
為驚玉貌郎君墜，
不得華軒更一嘶。

6 PEARL PARTED FROM PALM

Translucent, bright, and round, this perfect jewel lets
light shine through like a treasure in Crystal Palace.
A bit of dirt found its way in and marred its perfection,
for that it no longer lies in the palm where it nestled.

FLOATING ON CLOUDS

其六：珠離掌

皎潔圓明內外通，
清光似照水晶宮。
只緣一點玷相穢，
不得終宵在掌中。

7 FISH PARTED FROM POND

In this water I have swum and leaped for four, five autumns,
swishing my jeweled tail, playing among the fishing lines.
Quite by accident, I broke a gorgeous lotus from its stem,
now I am no longer allowed to frolic in the pure green pond.

其七：魚離池

跳躍深池四五秋，
常搖朱尾弄綸鈎。
無端擺斷芙蓉朵，
不得清波更一遊。

In the next poem, we are back at Witch Mountain where Songyu imagined that story of the goddess who came as "rain in the morning and cloud at night" and gave us the Chinese euphemism for intercourse forever after. The decline of the Kingdom of Chu was not an overnight affair, but after his rendezvous with the goddess, King Xiang was said to have neglected his duties, and gradually became dissipated, which then led to the fall of his kingdom. This history seems to keep repeating itself.

We have seen now how our poets are often inspired by the same ancient stories but touched in different ways. Xue Tao may have written this poem while she visited the temple in the poem, but we do not have to be literal about it, she may well have imagined herself visiting Songyu's fairytale world, and the whole scene may have been evoked for the sake of the last two lines. Being a courtesan herself, Xue Tao was surely sympathetic to all those courtesans at Chu who would have made themselves up every day, waiting, in vain, for their king to come to his senses.

ON VISITING A TEMPLE AT WITCH MOUNTAIN

Step into the poet's fairyland and hear the gibbons' wild shriek
coming out of the thick mist and the woodsy scent of these hills.
The scenery bears traces of Songyu's story, and sounds of water
cry out as if King Xiang is still sobbing after his goddess left him.
Night and day and day and night on the terrace of Witch Mountain,
they met in an embrace of cloud and rain, and for that, Chu was lost.
Saddened, I am touched by the many willows swaying before me,
imagining Chu courtesans painting their brows, waiting for their king.

FLOATING ON CLOUDS

謁巫山廟

亂猿啼處訪高唐，
路入煙霞草木香。
山色未能忘宋玉，
水聲猶是哭襄王。
朝朝夜夜陽台下，
為雨為雲楚國亡。
惆悵廟前多少柳，
春來空門畫眉長。

In the next two poems we find the goddess again. In "Peony," she compares the man who had to leave to the goddess, and in the Double Ninth poem, the poet herself is the goddess. Let us focus first on "Peony". Two stories are evoked in this poem. One is the Witch Mountain fable, and the other is the folktale about two Wuling men who met two goddesses on their way home one day, got married to them and only later returned home, by which time, many generations have passed. It is another Rip Van Winkle story. At first glance, it would seem to have the opposite outcome to the Witch Mountain story, as the men married the goddesses and stayed, while the mountain goddess left and never returned. On second look, however, the Wuling men, by staying with the goddesses had lost everything they had when they returned home. So, it, too, has a tragic outcome. Wuling, moreover, is where Tao Qian's "Peach Blossom Spring" is set. In other words, she is saying, "Once you leave here (paradise), you may never find your way back!"

Let us imagine she was thinking of Yuan Zhen as the peony, the young man who was as beautiful as the flower. We are used to thinking of men imagining women as flowers, but why shouldn't women imagine the men they admire to be like flowers?

MY CHINA IN TANG POETRY

Especially, in this case since the man is much younger than the woman. They had just met not long ago, fallen in love and now he had to go. He promised to come back, but she couldn't be sure. After all, he was just at the beginning of his pursuit of a government career. The "crimson petals" may also indicate that she had written this poem on that red flower colored "Xue Tao Note" which she sent to him. In the beginning of their affair, he may or may not have been married, but I am skeptical about her thinking that he would marry her. She was, at forty-one, not a foolish young girl any more, like the one who wrote the earlier poems, but who knows, love does crazy things to people, even to intelligent men and women.

PEONY

It was late spring last year when your crimson petals fell
and my tears fell on them even faster as we said goodbye.
I worry that you are like that goddess on Witch Mountain,
or perhaps our story will be like that of the Wuling men.
Even now, silently, your scent follows me wherever I go.
We used to have no need for words to express our love.
All I ask for is a pillow by your side again, and each night
we can exchange our longing one to another like before.

FLOATING ON CLOUDS

牡丹

去春零落暮春時，
淚濕紅箋怨別離。
常恐便同巫峽散，
因何重有武陵期？
傳情每向馨香得，
不語還應彼此知。
只欲欄邊安枕蓆，
夜深閒共說相思。

Let us then imagine he came back to her after leaving once or twice and was staying at the nunnery to study for the Imperial exam. He was staying for a while at the guest house. It was Chong Yang, the Double Ninth Festival, chrysanthemums were in bloom everywhere, both wild (on the mountains) and domestic (in the garden), and dogwood branches had been cut and readied for the hike and picnic, but it turned out to be a rainy day that year, so Xue Tao offered an alternative entertainment to hiking. The following are two poems, but they might as well have been two stanzas to the same poem. River City is another name for Chengdu. Also, the word "goddess," has come to mean "prostitute" in certain quarters these days because of the Witch Mountain Goddess's reputation.

ON A RAINY DOUBLE NINTH (two poems)
1

Ten thousand miles of panting wind tunneling through,
gray clouds coming with daybreak, shrouding River City.
There will be no hiking or picnic this year on Double Ninth.
A pity since everywhere the hills are covered in winter gold.

MY CHINA IN TANG POETRY

2

Dogwood branches have been prepared for this festival day, and the garden is filled with the fragrance of chrysanthemums. Perhaps a goddess will decide to pay you a visit if you wish hard enough: see if the pond is overcast and if it starts to rain.

九日遇雨二首
其一

萬里驚飆朔氣深，
江城蕭索晝陰陰。
誰憐不得登山去，
可惜寒芳色似金。

其二

茱萸秋節佳期阻，
金菊寒花滿院香。
神女欲來知有意，
先令雲雨暗池塘。

Soon he had to leave again, perhaps the Imperial Exam date had arrived. In any case, we know now that lover boy was to abandon her. The next poem, she tells us in the title, is written as four verses of a lyric. In other words, it may have been sung, accompanied by music.

FLOATING ON CLOUDS

SPRING VIEW IN FOUR VERSES

You're not here to admire them when flowers bloom.
You're not here with me to feel sad when they fall.
If you ask me when it is that I most long for you,
it is when flowers are in bloom and when they fall.

You tied grass knots for me to show your love,
to tell me that you appreciated my music.
Spring comes with sorrow, your voice cut off,
even birds are sad now, crying for each other.

A strong wind has risen, withering flowers.
Your return has moved further and further away.
Love knots have not tied your heart to mine,
I'm left with nothing but silly knots of grass.

Spring branches are still full of flowers,
and we are still far apart. In the morning,
the mirror shows tears running down my face.
Can the spring wind comprehend this sadness?

春望詞四首

花開不同賞，
花落不同悲。
欲問相思處，
花開花落時。

MY CHINA IN TANG POETRY

攬草結同心，
將以遺知音。
春愁正斷絕，
春鳥復哀吟。

風花日將老，
佳期猶渺渺。
不結同心人，
空結同心草。

那堪花滿枝，
翻作兩相思。
玉箸垂朝鏡，
春風知不知。

We will end this selection with the next three poems, probably written late in her life, after she had left the life of entertainment and retired to the hills. This is where the Wang Jiang Lou Park is built. People seem to play mahjong under the bamboo there these days. I think this might be a bit too noisy for Xue Tao.

In the next three poems, we can imagine that in the first poem "her heart is not yet like stilled water," 心如止水, meaning, hope has yet to be entirely extinguished. In the second poem, she is closer to detachment. In the third, she has arrived. At least, one would like to think that.

As asserted earlier, the Tang emperor's leaning towards Daoism does not negate his or anybody else's belief or study of Buddhism, even if the two religions are sometimes in competition and even at odds with each other. In this poem, Xue Tao is alluding to the Heart Sutra, the most recited of Buddhist sutras. It is believed that meditating on the color red will take one to the place where the delusion of attachment turns into the wisdom of discernment, to tell truth from fiction or fantasy. Wild geese and carps, you remember, are messengers.

BY THE RIVER

> A west wind rises. Suddenly pairs of wild geese appear in the sky.
> In this life, our hearts are two, each meditating on its own red hue.
> If I did not believe that these carps are true messengers from you,
> would I be standing here by the water, waiting, dreaming, hoping?

江邊

西風忽報雁雙雙，
人世心形兩自降。
不為魚腸有真訣，
誰能夢夢立清江。

WILLOW CATKINS

In the second month, willow catkins begin to appear.
Spring wind teases and tugs gently at people's clothes.
Don't be fooled by their playfulness, these things of spring
have no feelings, flying south, flitting north, they don't care.

MY CHINA IN TANG POETRY

柳絮

二月楊花輕復微，
春風搖盪惹人衣。
他家本是無情物，
一任南飛又北飛。

ROWING ON THE LOTUS POND

Down the stream come fisher boats, pressing lotuses close to the shore.
They call out news of the coming fall and that fish is plentiful this year.
Rabbits run past, birds zip by, people speak softly so as not to disturb
the scene of reds on the water. Somewhere, someone has started a song.

採蓮舟

風前一葉壓荷蕖，
解報新秋又得魚。
兔走烏馳人語靜，
滿溪紅袂棹歌初。

5

Liu Caichun 劉採春 (dates uncertain)
Singer, Actor

Chinese people seem to like to group things and people in pairs, twos or fours. So, just as there are "Four Great Beauties of China", there are "Four Great Female Talents of the Tang Dynasty", although one of them hardly wrote anything; at least we have no record of her writing, except for six poems attributed to her in the *Tang Poetry Collection*, which may or may not be reliable. She was, apparently, an excellent singer, though, and well-known to the literati in her day. Her name was Liu Caichun.

Since we have been on Yuan Zhen's case already about his relationship with Xue Tao, let me tell you right off the bat that some have said that he may have cost this talented singer her life. We know little of her as she was neither born into an official's family nor did she become a Daoist nun. She was born into a poor family. Fortunately for her, she had a beautiful voice, and she could act too. You might call her a pop singer of her day. She joined an acting troupe early and married another actor and together with his brother, formed an acting troupe of their own and traveled around putting on shows. The troupe became well known for putting on shows for and about the military. She wrote a series of songs, popularly known as "Missing My Man" 望夫歌" and they were so moving that there was hardly a dry

MY CHINA IN TANG POETRY

eye after her shows, especially those of the women whose sons and husbands have been hauled away by the army. Here are two verses, roughly translated from the first two lyrics. It is hard to convey their effectiveness without the music and her voice to convey them:

> I hate the waters of Rivers Qin and Wei,
> I loathe the boats that sail on its waves.
> They take my sons and my husband,
> year after year after years like lifetimes.
>
> Don't ever marry a merchant, all you'll have
> left would be those few pieces of gold coins
> for fortune-telling, and day in and day out
> you'll be mistaking other men's boats for theirs.

> 不喜秦淮水,
> 生憎江上船。
> 載兒夫婿去,
> 經歲又經年。
>
> 莫作商人婦,
> 金釵當卜錢。
> 朝朝江口望,
> 錯認幾人船。

From 820 to 829, Yuan Zhen, was sent to Yuezhou as a local official serving the district. He heard about Lui Caichun and invited her to perform for him. Afterwards, he wrote a poem praising her beauty and gave it to her as a gift; it generally described how beautiful her brows were, how elegant her movements and how alluring her voice. Since I do not find it particularly remarkable,

FLOATING ON CLOUDS

I have not translated it. As is so often the case, this next poem he wrote presents us with one of life's little ironies. Nobody can be entirely sure whether he wrote this poem for his wife, who died young, and with whom he may really have been in love, or whether it was for any of the women he may or may not have loved and abandoned or lost. The poem is from a set of mourning poems. They will all be in the chapter under his name in Volume III. The verse I am referring to is as follows:

> Having once sailed on the open sea, all bodies of water feels small to me.
> Having seen Witch Mountain clouds, no other cloud deserves the name.
> Were I to find myself among a million flowers, I would not care to look,
> perhaps this is half the result of studying the Dao, and half because of you.

曾經滄海難為水
除卻巫山不是雲
取次花叢懶回顧
半緣修道半緣君

The first two lines of this poem by our Lothario have been used by countless lovers to express their remembrance of love lost ever after. Since we now know that Yuan Zhen did look at other flowers after he wrote this poem, we cannot allow ourselves to be fooled.

According to hearsay, the poem he wrote Liu Caichun after she sang for him, so moved her that she left her husband and children and became his mistress. When he abandoned her, she committed suicide by throwing herself into a river.

6

Yu Xuanji 魚玄機 (844？- 871)
On Her Own

Yu Xuan Ji's birth name was You Wei, 幼薇, meaning "young rose or fern", her courtesy name is Hui Lan 蕙蘭, which means "orchid". Among the Four Talented Females, she is the most appreciated by Chinese historians and commentators, and therefore the most translated into English. As with Li Ye, her birth year is also vague, and she also had a sensational death. Thus, we know she died in 871, before she reached her thirtieth year. She, too, was executed, for the "lesser" crime of beating her maid to death in a jealous rage, (as opposed to the treasonous crime of insulting the emperor with verses like Li Ye).

She was born and bred in Chang'an. In those twenty-four or twenty-seven years of her short life, she experienced 1) the life of a talented young girl who met the famous poet Wen Tingyun 溫庭筠 when she was only ten and became his "age-forgotten friend" (that is, being friends without worrying about age differences); 2) at fourteen or sixteen, she became a married woman, albeit to a man who already had a wife, so she was a concubine; and 3) a Daoist nun and courtesan when the first wife could not stand having her in her house and kicked her out. She was around twenty at the time. And then, several years later, she became the afore-mentioned killer, an experience she did not have time to regret or write about.

In David Young's translation (in collaboration with Hsuan-chi Yu, *The Clouds Float North: The Complete Poems of Yu Xuan Ji* in the Wesleyan Poetry Series, published in 1998), is a succinct introduction to her and her poetry that is available online under the auspices of University of Virginia's "Chinese Text Initiative": https://cti.lib.virginia.edu/yu/yuintro.html. Curiously, Young does not mention Wen Tingyun and his friendship with Yu. He had her die at twenty-four.

As the story goes, Yu 魚 (unusual last name, meaning fish) was also a child prodigy, and her father, also a scholar who appreciated his daughter's talent, taught her poetry. Her poems were so good that her fame traveled and reached the ear of the poet-scholar-official, Wen Tingyun. His curiosity brought him to her house. On his way, he saw willow trees by the riverbank and catkins on the wind. So, when he arrived and met the child, he set her the topic, "Willows by the Riverbank" and asked for a poem. The following is what she came up with:

SONG OF WILLOWS BY THE RIVERBANK

Kingfisher green willows cover once naked riverbanks.
Dancing in the wind, they reach for buildings far away.
Their misty reflections on the autumn water multiply
catkins as they fall and fly, landing on fishermen's heads.
Ancient roots make good hiding places for fish to rest,
lower tree branches give shady shelter to visiting sails.
On windy, rainy nights, sighs and loud sobbing outside
wakes me from my dreams, shrouding the dark in sadness.

MY CHINA IN TANG POETRY

賦得江邊柳

翠色連荒岸，
煙姿入遠樓。
影鋪秋水面，
花落釣人頭。
根老藏魚窟，
枝底系客舟。
蕭蕭風雨夜，
驚夢復添愁。

Wen Tingyun was floored. She was beautiful too, but he restrained himself, a rare feat it seems in those days. He visited often, apparently, after that and became more of a mentor, to his credit, than a suiter. They exchanged many poems, and this, being her first relationship with an older man, she developed a bit of a crush, as we shall see from some of her poems sent to him. Soon, he left Chang'an on official business and resided in Xiangyang (Meng Haoran's hometown). The two continued to write each other until her untimely death.

Here are two of the many poems she sent to Wen, whom she addresses by his courtesy name, Feiqing, 飛卿. She does not hide her affection for him and is in fact rather bold in expressing her longing. In the first poem she might as well be proposing to him. In the second, she sounds every bit the neglected lover. We are told by some of his contemporaries that Wen was quite ugly on top of being so much older than her. She must have loved him purely for his poetry and was certainly not superficial in her appreciation of beauty.

"Looking for a place to rest" is a euphemism for a woman looking for a family to marry into. In this case, the tall "wutong tree" is Wen's family, somewhat higher on the social ladder than her own. Nonetheless, if he didn't think her status too low for him, then she could stop "circling the forest".

"Original Mind" 本來心 is a Buddhist expression describing the mind one is born with, the innocent mind with nothing in it, no knowledge, no bias, nothing, therefore free from desire and attachment, usually a good thing in that context, here, she is complaining. The "tides of fortune" encompasses the concept of the rise and fall of nations among other fortunes, but here, she is using it to apply to herself. Because of her intelligence, one often forgets how young she was.

SENT TO WEN FEIQING ON A WINTER NIGHT

To dispel these bitter thoughts, I looked for poems to read,
afraid of my cold quilt and the long night of sleeplessness.
The miserable wind is tossing dry leaves about in the yard.
Through my gauze window the sinking moon is just as sad.
Separated from you, my heart's desire is too far from reach.
Fortune has denied me all but this barren Original Mind.
Uncertain if the wutong is too high, or which tree is best,
I'm circling the forest like a bird looking for a place to rest.

冬夜寄溫飛卿

苦思搜詩燈下吟，
不眠長夜怕寒衾。
滿庭木葉愁風起，
透幌紗窗惜月沈。
疏散未閒終遂願，
盛衰空見本來心。
幽棲莫定梧桐處，
暮雀啾啾空繞林。

MY CHINA IN TANG POETRY

SENT TO FEIQING

Cacophonous crickets make noise on my stone steps.
Out in the courtyard, nothing but a chilly, misty blur.
Through the moonlight comes my neighbor's music.
It's not too dark to go upstairs for a view of the hills.
This straw mat is almost too cool now for the season;
my qin can convey only so many sad autumn feelings.
Are you too busy or too lazy to write letters anymore?
Will I have to find comfort in less comforting things?

寄飛卿

堦砌亂蛩鳴，
庭柯煙露清。
月中隣樂響，
樓上遠山明。
珍簟涼風著，
瑤琴寄恨生。
稽君懶書札，
底物慰秋情。

I'm calling the next poem "Xishi's Shrine" instead of following the Chinese exactly by calling it "Washer Maid's Shrine". We met Xishi quite a few times in Volume I with Li Bai's poems, and Wang Wei too wrote "A Xishi Song" (See p.64). Briefly, to refresh your memory, the Xishi story is part of a historical tale of two rival tribes or kingdoms, Wu 吳 and Yue 越, and their inter-generational wars. First, Yue won, and the King of Wu told his son Fuchai 夫差 that he must avenge him. Fuchai did: Goujian 勾踐, the son of the King of Yue lost to Fuchai 夫差, now the King of Wu, but then Fuchai became complacent, or overly ambitious, depending on interpretation, and eventually lost his kingdom to Yue.

Xishi 西施 was a washer maid of Yue who was discovered by General Fanli, 范蠡. One version of the story has it that he fell in love with her but sacrificed himself (and her) for their country, trained, and sent her to the enemy Kingdom of Wu as spy and enchantress. In this poem, Yu Xuanji emphasizes Xishi's power as enchantress and introduces another character to our continuing story. As mentioned in Volume I, one version of the legend has it that Xishi went off with Fanli after Yue won against Wu. Here, our poet chooses a different version of her fate. She has Fanli leaving the scene alone and leaves Xishi's fate to our imagination. Then, she introduces another character, that of Wu Zixu 伍子胥, into our consciousness. Note that this Wu 伍 is not the same word as the Wu 吳 of the Kingdom of Wu.

Wu Zixu's father and brother were both killed by the old king of Yue, Goujian's father, because of treacherous rumors and misunderstandings. Wu Zixu, the youngest son, escaped to the kingdom of Wu 吳, hoping one day to avenge his father and his brother. He became a very important strategist and adviser to Fuchai and helped him win against Goujian. After winning, however, Fuchai did not heed Wu Zixu's repeated advice to kill Goujian when he had the chance, and in the end, lost his kingdom to Yue. Wu Zixu died for the same reasons that his father and brother died, because of vicious rumors and innuendos against him. In his case, he was given "the gift of the sword" by Fuchai to kill himself (sometimes it's the gift of poison, and always called a gift if it's given by a king or emperor.) Before he died, he requested that his eyes be gouged out and hung on 諸暨 Zhuji's city wall so that he could see the ruin of Wu when it came to pass. All of that is alluded to in this little poem. When historical tales become as well-known as this one, poets can allude to people and events in them and use them like a communal vocabulary.

MY CHINA IN TANG POETRY

Now that you share this vocabulary, the "green hills of Zhu Luo" is the final notation you'll need for the poem. Zhu Luo 苎萝 is Xishi's birthplace.

XISHI'S SHRINE

Wu and Yue left war stories and strategies galore.
Thanks to Xishi, the washer maid, peace was made.
A pair of dimples, a turn of her head, a smile,
and well-trained warriors laid down their spears.
His mission accomplished, Fanli chose a hermit's life.
Wu Zixu was ignored and given the gift of the sword.
All that's left are Zhuji's city wall,
and Xishi's green hills of Zhu Luo.

浣紗廟

吳越相謀計策多，
浣紗神女已相和。
一雙笑靨才回面，
十萬精兵盡倒戈。
范蠡功成身隱遁，
伍胥諫死國消磨。
只今諸暨長江畔，
空有青山號苎萝。

Back to Yu Xuanji's own story. Wen Tingyun, having magnanimously kept her at arm's length, associating with her as her poetry mentor instead of lusting after her person, handed her over to a much younger man he thought was an upstanding scholar official. The man's name was Li Ji. He had just won the top spot in the Imperial Exam when he came by to visit the older poet and was introduced to this immortal-like beauty and talented young poet. How could he not fall for her? And for her part, this promising young scholar was too good an opportunity to miss. She was grateful to her teacher for the introduction and fell in love with the young man. They soon tied the knot. She may have known, and Wen may have known, and surely Li Ji himself knew that he already had a wife, but in Tang China, even though a man could take no more than one wife, he could have as many concubines as he could afford. In other words, Li Ji was marrying Yu Xuanji into his household as a concubine.

In the household, the wife had all legal rights. Concubines, on the other hand, had almost no power. They must obey the mistress. Even their children called the mistress mother and there was only one mother per household. The status of concubines was not much higher than that of the maid servants; they were both slaves and could be bought and sold. In this case, Li Ji, the husband, was supposed to have truly loved our poet, but by all accounts, the woman he married as wife was fierce and jealous. So, when she said Yu could no longer stay after he brought her home with him only for a short time, he had to let her go. Coward that he was, he tricked our poet, telling her she was going to a nunnery, temporarily, and that he would come to get her later. I have to keep reminding myself she was a teenager when she first met her future husband and was wed only for two, or at most, three years, and sharing him with other women at that. I am not excusing her for the eventual beating and death of her maid, even if beatings by wives on concubines and concubines on maids were not uncommon, but this whole mess and injustice does make one's blood boil.

The next two "Farewell Poems" are really two poems and sometimes split up and placed far apart in selections of her writings. I am putting them together because they are so similar in

MY CHINA IN TANG POETRY

style as well as content. I am imagining that they were addressed to her new husband who may have left on a short trip or left to go home in preparation to fetch her later on. She sounds, however, so unsure of his return that they may have been written before they were married, although being "married" meant little when applied to a concubine. You can decide where the two poems fit best in her time with Zi'an, Li Yi's courtesy name.

In the second of the two poems, she uses the cloud metaphor for the one who has gone away. "Clouds," are often used to signify wanderers because they drift and come and go from nowhere to nowhere. Also, when the wanderer is a man, which is almost always the case, he could be the counterpart of "rain," at least just as mysterious. For "immortal lover" in the Chinese I have translated "abiding love." The yang-bird is the counterpart of the yuan-bird of the pair of Mandarin ducks, called the yuan-yang birds in Chinese. They are often embroidered on blankets for newlyweds.

TWO FAREWELL POEMS
I

We were happy and contented all these nights.
Who knew my abiding love would leave me?
While I slept, he drifted away with the clouds.
Wild moths throw themselves at my dying lamp.

II

Sailing along on the gentle waves, aimlessly,
once it leaves, a cloud will never come back.
Travelers go where the spring wind blows,
The yang-bird is left here, her flock has flown.

FLOATING ON CLOUDS

送別 二首
其一

秦樓幾夜愜心期，
不料仙郎有別離。
睡覺莫言雲去處，
殘燈一盞野蛾飛。

其二

水柔逐器知難定，
雲出無心肯再歸。
惆悵春風楚江暮，
鴛鴦一隻失羣飛。

The sound of pounding paddles, or women washing clothes at the river, is the trope used to express how women, usually women who were left at home, long for their men who were not. We have seen this quite a few times before.

SENT TO THE OTHER SIDE OF THE HAN RIVER TO ZI'AN

River south, river north, I gaze upstream, you gaze down.
You think of me, I long for you, chanting one to the other.
Yuan-yang ducks snuggle in warm sandbanks.
Water birds play around in kumquat groves.
Misty water carries songs whispered in the twilight.
At the crossing, moonbeams are slowly sinking.
My love for you can travel ten thousand miles
even without the urging on of pounding paddles.

MY CHINA IN TANG POETRY

隔漢江寄子安

江南江北愁望，
相思相憶空吟。
鴛鴦暖臥沙浦，
鸂鶒閑飛橘林。
煙裏歌聲隱隱，
渡頭月色沈沈。
含情咫尺千里，
況聽家家遠砧。

In the next poem, the mention of the orchids dying and coming back to life alludes to her courtesy name which means orchid, and that spring wind coming from the east in China, is personified as male, or, in this case, Zi'an.

A LETTER TO ZI'AN

A thousand cups of wine will not wash away my sorrow.
Drunk but not drunk enough to untie these knots of parting.
Orchids have died back to the ground till springtime comes,
only willow catkins see you off all the way along the river.
Clouds gathering and spreading wherever the wind blows, but
love, like the river, must never forget to flow back to the sea.
I know you'll be gone for all this season of blooming,
but I'm not going to shut myself in, drunk in the tower.

FLOATING ON CLOUDS

寄子安

醉別千卮不浣愁，
離腸百結解無由。
蕙蘭銷歇歸春圃，
楊柳東西絆客舟。
聚散已悲雲不定，
恩情須學水長流。
有花時節知難遇，
未肯厭厭醉玉樓。

The context of the following poem tells us it was written in 859 or thereabouts. She was on her way to the nunnery in the south, in Jiangling. One wonders if he received any of these poems or did his jealous wife intercept them all? Also, there is some question as to whether this Jiangling is in the north or another river on the southern banks of the Yangtze). The description I give in the first line for the maples is from "thousands over tens of thousands of branches" in the Chinese. I did not use the exact same words but translated the image. The second half of the poem echoes the conclusion to Bai Juyi's great love song, the famous "Song of Everlasting Sorrow" or "Curse of Passion" as I rendered it in Volume I, Chapter One.

GAZING SADLY ON JIANGLING, SENT TO ZI'AN

Like a sparsely woven mat, maple branches crisscross in the sky,
Looking out from the bridge: returning sails play hide-and-seek.
My thoughts of you are like the West Lake waters, flowing
east, without a break, all day, all night, with no end in sight.

MY CHINA IN TANG POETRY

江陵愁望寄子安

楓葉千枝復萬枝，
江橋掩映暮帆遲。
憶君心似西江水，
日夜東流無歇時。

WITH SPRING APPROACHING, SENT TO ZI'AN

Climbing up the steep and rickety steps of this mountain path is not so hard, what's harder is the thought of being without you.
Melting ice in distant caves makes tinkling music like your voice.
Snowy mountain peaks remind me of your stately, elegant poise.
Excessive drinking and popular songs are not worth hankering after.
Idle guests and playing chess late into the night are things of the past.
Our vows are strong and enduring as pines growing through the rocks.
Patiently I'll wait for the day when we can fly wing-to-wing once more.
I must make this journey in these last days of winter all by myself,
and when the moon is full again, my one wish will surely come true.
I had nothing meaningful to give you when we said goodbye.
All I have now is this poem from my heart, still wet with tears.

FLOATING ON CLOUDS

春情寄子安

山路欹斜石磴危，不愁行苦苦相思。
冰銷遠硐憐清韻，雪遠寒峯想玉姿。
莫聽凡歌春病酒，休招閒客夜貪棋。
如松匪石盟長在，比翼連襟會肯遲。
雖恨獨行冬盡日，終期相見月圓時。
別君何物堪持贈，淚落晴光一首詩。

"Brooding in my Boudoir" is a common title for poems of women waiting for their husband or lover to come. Miwu 蘪蕪 is a fragrant herb that women collect and is supposedly a fertility drug. When it is found in poetry it usually refers to spousal relationships. The pounding of laundry paddles is again another reminder of missing husbands. In this case, depending on when she wrote this poem and who she's writing about, the "husband" could be real or imagined or anticipatory, because after Zi'an sent her to the nunnery, he never came back and she then became a courtesan. Perhaps she was still hoping he'd come back for her, or thought maybe someone else might take her to their home, even if it would be as another concubine? After all, she was still in her twenties. Can you imagine? She's been through so much already.

BROODING IN MY BOUDOIR

I came in with an armful of miwu as the sun was slanting west,
and heard the news that my neighbor's husband has come home.
On the day you left, wild geese had just started flying north,
this morning I saw the first ones returning south to me.
Spring coming, autumn going, longing is longing still,
Autumn leaving, spring returning with fewer letters from you.

MY CHINA IN TANG POETRY

I keep my doors closed most days; nobody ever comes.
The only intruder is the incessant pounding of laundry paddles.

閨怨

蘼蕪盈手泣斜暉，
聞道鄰家夫婿歸。
別日南鴻纔北去，
今朝北雁又南飛。
春來秋去相思在，
秋去春來信息稀。
扃閉朱門人不到，
砧聲何事透羅幃。

LINES JOTTED DOWN IN LATE SPRING

Few visitors come to my humble door at the end of the alley.
Only in dreams does my lover heed my pleading for him to stay.
The scent of silk gowns drifting by makes me wonder who is having a party?
Music and singing are in the autumn wind. Where is it coming from?
Drumbeats from a nearby street rudely wake me from my morning sleep,
out in the courtyard, chattery magpies confuse my sad, spring mood.
How is it possible to pursue daily affairs with peace of mind?
Might as well untether my boat and let it sail freely to the sea.

FLOATING ON CLOUDS

暮春即事

深巷窮門少侶儔，
阮郎唯有夢中留。
香飄羅綺誰家席？
風送歌聲何處樓？
街近鼓鼙喧曉睡，
庭閑鵲語亂春愁。
安能追逐人間事，
萬里身同不繫舟。

Leaving the ground unswept is supposed to bring home whoever is away as quickly as possible. Smooth green moss on the doorstep means no one has visited.

YOU WERE ON MY MIND, A LETTER

My regrets are all played out in the song I just strummed.
I kept my feelings hidden, lest you think me too forward.
Had I known we would end up just making cloud and rain,
I would not have let my orchid heart respond so recklessly.
Too gaudy those new spring flowers, opening to my face.
Tell me it's the country's business you are leaving me for,
I won't get in your way. Noble pines and elegant cassias,
those are things the whole world respects and pursues.
Moonlight shows smooth green moss on my doorsteps, only
distant singing voices through thick bamboo reaches my ear.
Red leaves pave the ground outside my door. Let them be,
as I wait for the one who knows my voice to come to me.

MY CHINA IN TANG POETRY

感懷寄人

恨寄朱弦上，含情意不任。
早知雲雨會，未起蕙蘭心。
灼灼桃兼李，無妨國士尋。
蒼蒼松與桂，仍羨世人欽。
月色苔階淨，歌聲竹院深。
門前紅葉地，不掃待知音。

And here's a rare moment of tranquility to take us out. We can imagine her floating on a flatboat on clouds reflected on the water.

ON A SUMMER DAY, LIVING IN THE MOUNTAINS

Living like an immortal up high on the mountain,
flowers flourish all around me without bother.
In the front porch I hang my coat on a tree branch,
I drink wine from cups floating on spring water.
My footpath turns into a forest of wild bamboo.
Silk robes are casually draped over stacks of books.
You can often find me lounging on my flatboat,
trusting to the gentle wind to blow me where it will.

FLOATING ON CLOUDS

夏日山居

移得仙居此地來，
花叢自遍不曾栽。
庭前亞樹張衣桁，
坐上新泉泛酒杯。
軒檻暗傳深竹徑，
綺羅長擁亂書堆。
閒乘畫舫吟明月，
信任輕風吹卻回。

Endnote: Verse Forms

The oldest book of Chinese poetry is the *Shijing*, 詩經, often translated as the *Book of Songs*, mainly folk songs collected from as early as the first millennium BCE. Confucius (551 BCE-479 BCE) is said to have been its final editor. Poetry is generally referred to as *shi*, and *jing* means collection. The vocabulary and culture of the *Shijing* is associated with the northern region of China. The dominant line of a poem in the *Shijing* is four characters.

In the south comes another important collection of early poetry called the *Chu Ci* 楚辭 (dated back to The Warring States, ca. 475-221 BCE). The *Chu Ci* is made up of several books, the most important of which is the *Li Sao* 離騷, a lament attributed to Qu Yuan 屈原 (340 BCE-278 BCE). The poems in the *Chu Ci* vary in line lengths and their imagery is associated with the State of Chu 楚. Much flora and fauna are found in poetry both north and south.

During the Han Dynasty 漢 (206 BCE-227 CE) the classic *shi* 詩 with its four-character lines was revived, and a new development of poems of five-and seven-character lines emerged. In addition, there had been a Music Bureau, or department of music in court found as early as the mythical government of Huang Di, 黃帝, who has been credited with starting a whole slew of things, including astronomy, math, writing characters, sericulture, musical laws and a Chinese version of football, the taming of wild beasts, the string instrument, guqin, and even invention of upper and lower garments and the weaving and dyeing of cloth. There is little documentary evidence though that the Music Bureau existed until the Qin 秦 (221-205 BCE) and into the Han dynasties.

Some Verse Forms Popularly Used In the Tang Dynasty (618–907)

The Tang Dynasty is often referred to as the Golden Age of Poetry in China. Poets of this period freely adopted and refined past verse forms and new forms were crystallized. The *lushi*, 律詩, was perfected early in the dynasty. It is a five- or seven-character, eight-line composition with prescribed tonal and rhyme schemes, calling for parallel structure in the middle, that is, second and third couplets. It is often translated as "regulated verse" in English. Then came the *jueju* 绝句, which was an outgrowth of the *lushi*. This is a four-line, five- or seven-character poem. That means it is half a *lushi*, and thus, is often translated as "curtailed" or "truncated" verse. The tonal patterns of the *lushi* are kept but the parallel structure is made optional, although the couplet remains foundational to the form. We think of it as a *lushi* cut short. The aesthetics of the *jueju* are similar to the Japanese haiku (which was inspired by the *jueju*) in that it invites one to contemplate and further ruminate on its meaning as it ends and is judged by its economy and suggestiveness. The *pailu* 排律 also started to emerge. This is a long form of the *lushi*, and length is not prescribed, so long as it runs in couplets. These are all called New Style Verse 近體詩 in the Tang dynasty.

Then, there is the *gushi*, 古詩, with *gu* meaning "old-style" or "ancient" and *shi* meaning "verse." It was the *yuefu* 樂府 that led the way to its development with the broader use of rhyme and fewer metrical restrictions. In the Tang dynasty, its use was revived and is differentiated from regulated verse by not following, or even deliberately violating, the rules of the *lushi*.

The *yuefu* itself was a form of poetry derived from folk-ballads. Yue fu means "music/bureau," and the poetic form is named after the governmental department of music by that name. (The character "*fu*" here is not to be confused with another word, "*fu*,"

MY CHINA IN TANG POETRY

賦 of the same sound but not the same tone, and a different word altogether, meaning "ode" or "rhapsody.") The Music Bureau in the Han dynasty collected folksongs. Confucius said that folk songs represented the voice of the people. The musical scores from these songs were used for ceremonial occasions at court as well. This collection of folk poetry from the Han dynasty serves as the basis of the *yuefu* form. These poems consisted of lines of varying lengths and broke away from the older four-character line by their use of the five-character. Tang poets imitated these *yuefu* ballads and made up their own poems accordingly. Du Fu and Bai Juyi were both promoters of this form.

Poets and Dates

In Volume I: *Superstars*
Li Bai or Li Bo (Li Po)   701 – 762
Du Fu (Tu Fu)   712 – 770

In Volume II: *Floating on Clouds*
Meng Haoran (Meng Hao-jan)   689/91 – 740
Wang Wei (Wang Wei)   699 – 761
Li Ye (Li Ye)   737? – 784
Xue Tao (Hsueh T'ao)   768 – 831
Liu Caichun (Liu Ts'ai – ts'un)   uncertain
Yu Xuanji (Yu Hs'uan-chi)   844 – 871

In Volume III: *Friends and Lovers*
Liu Zongyuan (Liu Chungyuan)   773 – 819
Liu Yuxi (Liu Yushi)   772 – 842
Bai Juyi (Po Chu-i)   772 – 846
Yuan Zhen (Yuan Chen)   779 – 831
Li He (Li Ho)   790 – 816
Du Mu (Tu Mu)   803 – 852
Li Shangyin (Li Shang-yin)   812 – 858

Acknowledgements

Many of these poems have been with me since childhood, but it was in telling my mother's story after her passing that I felt the urgency of putting together these translations for others. At the same time, my friend, Virginia Raymond, suggested that we start a writing group. Nancy Vine Durling immediately responded, and since then, the three of us, with occasional visitors, have been meeting sporadically for reading and writing sessions. Virginia, an attorney and Latin American literature professor, Nancy, a medieval French scholar and translator, and I come from entirely different backgrounds, bringing fresh perspectives to each other's work, both sympathetic and critical. This variety of input reminds me of the poetry and translation workshops at Princeton where, as an undergraduate, I began to develop an eye and an ear for writing beyond myself. I must especially acknowledge my teachers, John Peck, Edmund Keeley, and Charles Tomlinson, who took my writing seriously, more so than I could have done myself, and gave me the confidence and critical training that never left me. I must also thank all the students who participated in the translation workshops I attended throughout my years at Princeton, all coming with different languages and cultures, who shared their work with me as I with them, as we pounced on each other with youthful criticism and appreciation. Among these cohorts, Nadia Benabid has remained a staunch comrade in verse long after we both left graduate school. A big thank you is due also to the Fates who led me to Earnshaw Books and the "yes" from Mr. Graham Earnshaw, whose keen eye saw the merits of this series of Tang poems and helped me launch them into the world. And, I am in debt to to my friends, Jim Earl and Laura Gibbs, who have read many of these pages and hunted down my stray commas and miscellaneous mistakes.

To my mother, who sowed the seeds of love of classical Chinese poetry in me, and to David, my life-support and partner, I have no words that can fully express my gratitude. To Su Zhong, the first person I turn to whenever I have Chinese questions, and my high school and kindergarten classmates from Hong Kong scattered all over the world who have remained close and encouraging; to Mrs. O'Connell, the fiery speech teacher at Diocesan Girls' School who first taught me how to breathe and dance to the rhythms of English poetry, how can I thank you for the gifts you have given me?

In addition, there have been sympathetic listeners that kept me afloat, both friends and strangers, some of whom are no longer with us. I am grateful to them all. At a few junctures of my writing life when I might have given up, encouragement came my way from such writers and critics as James J.Y. Liu, who was Yvonne Sung-Sheng Chang's mentor and who led her to me for the translation of Wang Wen-Hsing's important Modernist novel, *Jia Bian (Family Catastrophe)*, and Wang Wen-Hsing himself; Stephen Soong, who held up an issue of *Renditions* from going to press in order to wait for my small contribution, and who was generous enough to say that he heard the Chinese poems in my English, which, apparently, was a new experience for him; and Joseph S.M. Lau, who, sadly, passed away recently, and who also showed an interest in my translations and gave me the chance to work on some stories he collected in the *Columbia Anthology of Modern Chinese Literature*. I am grateful also to have met all my students through the years, from the one who said I was the only professor who kept him awake in class, to Robert Emerson who told me my poetry "kicks ass," and Beatrice Halbach-Singh who has become a close friend and enthusiastic listener, and all my readers wherever you are, and particularly the anonymous reader, "James," who reviewed *A River in Springtime* on "Goodreads" and called it "masterful."

Finally, to my daughter, Anne 天菲, who is the guru in my life, and my son, Zachary 甘苇, prominent in my mind as representing future generations in the Chinese Diaspora as well as poetry lovers everywhere, this is for you.

Epilogue

Growing up in Hong Kong, I did not do well in Chinese classes, and often received "big eggs", meaning zeroes, for Chinese "dictation" In this context, dictation means writing out assigned texts for memorization at home, and then writing them out in class, usually from classical Chinese poetry. In addition, such "dictations" had to be done with Chinese ink brushes, not an easy task for little hands to accomplish. Being neither studious nor particularly good at rote learning, I have no fond memories of such endeavors. On the other hand, I was fortunate to have a mother who loved the Chinese classics and would "sing" or "chant" poems and tell stories from them to me, and I absorbed by osmosis. It was not until I left the British colony for college that I discovered Chinese classical poetry for myself. Or you might say, when what I absorbed was given space to bloom.

My favorite poems were from the Tang and Song periods, and my love was discovered through English translation exercises. These exercises began at the Creative Writing workshops ran by the poet John Peck when I was an undergraduate at Princeton, and I continued taking these workshops as a graduate student under such poets as Edmund Keeley and Charles Tomlinson. I shall forever be grateful to them for what they sparked and helped nurture in me. In these workshops, I learned to borrow voices, making English poetry through listening to ghosts, the ancient Chinese poets whom my mother had sung to me all those years ago. Eventually, translation became an integral part of my work as a writer.

Translations follow originals. The music, images, and ideas

MY CHINA IN TANG POETRY

in the Chinese poems I translated were not of my own creation, did not come out of my own experience. Still, the more I wrote and translated the more I came to realize the understanding translation demands is not so different from the discoveries that grew out of my own writings. In other words, all writing is translation, from thoughts to words, and all translations, especially of poetry, are works of creative writing even though reading and understanding some other person's work and his or her culture precede the translator's creation. Translation is both greedy and generous, it wishes to appropriate as it wants to share and disseminate.

Let me now turn the coin onto its other side. The expression "lost in translation" acknowledges that not everything in one culture or language can be brought into another language or culture. Translation is, if not impossible, quixotic. I do not, however, agree with those who think that what comes across in translation only reveals that which cannot be translated, which is, after all what the phrase, "lost in translation" usually implies, that is, the failure of translation. Clearly, more is demanded of the reader of translations, just as more is demanded of the citizen of one culture to engage with those of other cultures. One must first be willing to take the leap of imagination into another world, and often, another period of time, in order to be a successful reader of translations. On the other hand, the more different the culture, the more one may be looking for differences, surprises, strangeness even. Perhaps that is why so many translations of Chinese classical poems especially have been allowed, even encouraged, to sound strange, foreign, and sometimes, weird, even nonsensical. Let me assure you that although there are Chinese poets who endeavor to "make it new" and surprise readers in their own culture with experimentation and refreshing choices, Chinese poetry is no more awkward or nonsensical than

English poetry. In other words, I am asking you to recognize poor expressions and bad poetry for what they are, and not expect or excuse them just because they are found in translations. To do so is to disrespect the art of translation, to denigrate the challenge it poses.

Since our world has simultaneously expanded and shrunk, I shall not belabor the point about the importance of cultural exchange and exposure. The shortcut to the heart of Chinese culture is through its classics. As the popular Chinese saying goes, "to the people, food is heaven." Let me add that classical poetry is second in importance to the Chinese people only to its cuisine. Chinese people everywhere quote from classical Chinese poetry, both to express themselves and to impress others. Lines from the Tang poet Li Bai's poem, "The Road to Shu is Hard," showed up in a popular rap performance in China not so long ago. There is even a rock band named Tang Dynasty in China. Classical Chinese poetry, especially Tang poetry, is very much a part of contemporary Chinese life. Beyond prosperity and power, the Tang dynasty is judged as significant also because of its receptive and adventurous characteristics. It is, as Mark Edward Lewis calls it, *China's Cosmopolitan Empire*, (The Belknap Press of Harvard University Press, 2012).

Few will disagree that the two giants or superstars of Tang poetry are Li Bai and Du Fu (also known as Li Po and Tu Fu in previous translations). There are many translations of their works into other languages, especially into English. Why, then, do I find it necessary to translate these poets again? My first answer is that translation is a performance art, and as with any great piece of music, each performance, especially the better ones, will have its own contributions to make. The second reason is that although there are many prose translations of these poems, and some in verse as well, many of these poems

MY CHINA IN TANG POETRY

are still waiting to be "rescued," to use David Young's reasoning in his *Du Fu: A Life in Poetry* (Knopf, 2008). When the Modernist poet Ezra Pound spoke of "making it [poetry] new", he meant that translating another culture's poetry can be used to refresh or transform one's own culture and poetry. Some poets have even "made [their own] poetry new" with no knowledge of the language from which they were translating. Pound himself, working from a crib, without knowing Chinese at the time, had done a better job than sinologists or Chinese translators with "The River Merchant's Wife", a poem by Li Bai, whom he called by his Japanese name, Rihaku. To give any translation a fair hearing, we must remember that translation is not a secondary art but a performance art.

Music, image, meaning, context, and culture are all important to poetry, and of all these elements, music is the hardest to convey. The task I set for myself is to do the best I can with the music I hear in the original Chinese poems, which I hear in Cantonese, and bring it over into my English translations as poetry. At the turn of the last century, the Chinese translations into English, whether in Britain or in America, tended to be too sing-songy or tried too hard to force a rhyme. After Pound and the Imagists and their efforts to "make it new", English translations from the Chinese have tended towards directness or experimentation. The better poets who translate today have managed to avoid fussiness, archaic expressions, passive descriptions and the not-so-subtle rhymes and rhythms in their work. The voice of the poet-translator, however, often takes precedence over the original poet's voice, so that poems from different Chinese poets sound alike in translations done by the same English or American poet. In such cases, the poems that result should more accurately be called "appropriations" or "conversations" rather than translations. An appropriation is the result of the poet taking a Chinese poem, mixing it with his or her own experience of a similar sentiment, tailoring it to suit her or his own feel of it, and cutting or building a new poem out of it. That seems to be acceptable these days, and some interesting pieces have come from the practice, but I cannot agree with calling this exercise translation or a faithful rendition of the original.

With that, I go back to my starting point. Translations follow originals. The creativity in this act is different though no less demanding than original compositions. Translators are obliged to be true to the original even as they make the most of their own resources. To appropriate without being faithful is to circumvent the demands of the art of translation. As I see it, my role as translator is not to give my voice to the original poet, but to borrow as I lend, that is, to reproduce in English with my ventriloquist's skill the voice I hear in the Chinese, and to place again the poem where I found it, in its historical and cultural contexts as best I can. It is my duty, in translating, to attempt to differentiate each individual poet's style one from the other. I am helped in this last challenge by the Chinese poet's own choice of form and content, as well as by his or her own personality and the stories they tell. Those interested in prosody should consult my chapter on "Verse Forms" at the end of each volume.

My China in Tang Poetry is the culmination of all the above discoveries, driven not only by my own love of the stories and poems but also by my desire to make what I know and love accessible to others who have no Chinese, at least, no classical Chinese and therefore have no way into that world. This series is my offer to take you with me to visit my ghosts.

About The Author

Susan Wan Dolling is a Chinese American writer who was born in Hong Kong, attended the Diocesan Girls' School, studied in Japan, and graduated from Princeton University with an AB in English and Creative Writing PhD in Comparative Literature. She has taught English and Literature at Fordham University and Chinese Literature at the University of Texas at Austin. Her translations of modern Chinese literature and classical Chinese poetry can be found in such publications as *Another Chicago Magazine, Poetry Magazine, Words Without Border, Two Lines, The Columbia Anthology of Modern Chinese Literature,* and *Renditions.* Her translation of Wang Wen-Hsing's Modernist novel, *Family Catastrophe* is in University of Hawaii Press's Fiction from Modern China Series. *Superstars, Floating on Clouds* and *Friends and Lovers,* the three volumes of stories, readings, and translations in the series, *My China in Tang Poetry,* was published in 2024 by Earnshaw Books. Most recently, she and her cello teacher, Dr. Chi-Hui Kao, has formed a musical duo called "Note After Note." For more on Susan and her work, please visit www.susanwandolling.com.

www.ingramcontent.com/pod-product-compliance
Lightning Source LLC
LaVergne TN
LVHW010328070526
838199LV00065B/5686